Marvin Waidelich 12/15/87

Recollections
Of a Mint Director

Recollections
Of a Mint Director

———

By Frank A. Leach

Bowers and Merena Galleries, Inc.
Wolfeboro, New Hampshire

ISBN 0-943161-01-0 (pbk.)

Recollections of a Mint Director
By Frank A. Leach

The following text, except for the new foreword by Q. David Bowers, is reprinted on a facsimile basis from *Recollections of a Newspaperman*, by Frank A. Leach, published by Samuel Levinson, San Francisco, 1917. The portion reprinted here appeared in the original text from pages 289 to 406.

Foreword Copyright 1987 Bowers and Merena Galleries, Inc.
First Printing; 2,000 copies
Published by Bowers and Merena Galleries, Inc.,
Box 1224, Wolfeboro, NH 03894

Contents

Foreword ....page 7
Chapter 1 ....page 11
Chapter 2 ....page 35
Chapter 3 ....page 93
Index ....page 133

Foreword

By Q. David Bowers, 1987

In 1982, while doing research for my *United States Gold Coins: An Illustrated History* book, Kenneth Hallenbeck loaned me a rare volume, *Recollections of a Newspaperman*, by Frank A. Leach, published in San Francisco in 1917. So far as I was aware at the time, the extensive information given concerning United States coins in the volume was new to the numismatic fraternity. At the time of publication years earlier, the book was not distributed in numismatic channels.

In 1987, while scanning a list of books for sale in an antiquarian bookseller's publication, I chanced upon a description of *Recollections of a Newspaperman*, lost no time in ordering it, and was rewarded a week or so later by a package containing a nice copy.

Frank Aleamon Leach was a native of Auburn, New York, having been born there on August 19, 1846, a descendant of an old New England family. In 1852 he relocated with his family in California, making the trip by steamer from New York City to Nicaragua, by mule across land through tropical forests, and then again by steamer up the Pacific coast to San Francisco. The first steamer called for on the Pacific leg of the journey was destroyed by fire, necessitating a wait for 30 days until another could be secured. By that time, the embarkation dock was crowded, and space on the new steamer was at a premium. Overloaded, the vessel took more than two weeks to reach San Francisco.

Leach settled with his family in Sacramento, where his father, having come two years earlier, was already engaged in the business of bottling soda water, the first such facility in the city.

In 1859, a decade before the completion of the transcontinental railroad, Frank Leach returned with his mother to Auburn to attend a family reunion. Retracing their earlier route, the pair went by steamer from San Francisco to the Isthmus of Panama, then crossed land, and on the eastern side took the steamer *Star of the West* for New York. After a stay in Auburn, Frank and his mother went in the autumn of 1860 to St. Johns, New Brunswick, to spend the winter with an aunt and uncle. After several other extended stops, they returned to California. In 1866 he became a publisher of the Napa *Reporter*, relocating in 1867 to Vallejo, where he

Recollections of a Mint Director

produced a weekly paper later known as the *Evening Chronicle*. Attracted by Oakland, the city across the bay from San Francisco, Leach sold the *Evening Chronicle* and founded the Oakland *Evening Enquirer*, which he operated until 1897, when President William McKinley appointed him to the post of superintendent of the San Francisco Mint. His efforts met with commendation, and in September 1907 President Theodore Roosevelt named him to be director of the United States Mint, with offices in Washington, D.C., supervising the production of the Philadelphia Mint as well as the various branches. He remained in that post until 1909, when he resigned to assume the presidency of the People's Water Company of Alameda and Contra Costa counties, California.

In 1917, Frank A. Leach completed his memoirs, covering what he described as a life experience of 65 years in California, connected with the pioneer days of the state, and fraught with incidents and events of interest and observations of historical value. The manuscript was originally intended for the perusal of his four sons—Frank, Abraham P., Edwin R., and Harry, whom he had by Mary Louise Powell, whom he married on December 1, 1870. "[This will] explain the peculiar phraseology in some of the passages where the writer appears as addressing his sons, a form which might seem out of place in a book written solely for the public eye," Leach noted.

The significance of the present text to the numismatist is stated succinctly by a paragraph extracted from the pages to follow: "It was my privilege, as superintendent of the Mint, to participate in the administration of one of the most interesting eras of the coinage history of our country. In this was embraced the record of the greatest volume of gold coinage; the introduction of the Philippine coinage; the radical change in designs of our gold coins; the adoption of the new electrolytic method of refining; and the first introduction of improved machinery and methods in coinage operations. In short, these were the years of greatest activity of the mints of the United States."

The reader will learn what happened to the San Francisco Mint during the Great Earthquake of 1906. A behind-the-scenes account of the creation of the famous MCMVII coinage furnishes what is the most complete contemporary record available today of the production of what many have described as America's most artistic coin design. Numerous other incidents will shed light on the operation of the San Francisco Mint, the Philadelphia Mint, and American coinage operations during this pivotal time in numismatic history.

—Q. David Bowers
October 21, 1987

Frank A. Leach

Chapter 1

In the Service of the Government

It was about this time, in May, 1897, after the inauguration of President McKinley, that I was greatly surprised to receive a telegram from Washington, signed by Congressman Hilborn, informing me that I was the choice of the delegation for the position of Superintendent of the United States mint in San Francisco, and desiring to know if I would accept the office. After taking a day to consider the matter, I decided to accept, concluding that the appointment would make it easier for me to get out of the newspaper business, and I wired an acceptance. I was appointed on the recommendation of Senator Perkins, and confirmed by the Senate in the month of June of that year, but I did not present my commission until August 1, that my predecessor, Honorable John Daggett, might fill out a four years' term of office. I found the duties to be agreeable and the work most interesting in character, which made me more anxious to be rid of the newspaper business, that I might give my whole attention to the new occupation. The opportunity came within a very short time. I sold the paper to G. B. Daniels and turned over my stock to him. It was with some feelings of regret, however, that I surrendered the property I had worked so hard to build up, and especially did I feel sadness in severing the intimate and close relations that had existed for years between myself and my loyal, zealous, and able co-laborers. However, the paper had accomplished the work it had set out to do, and I felt at liberty to turn it over to the control of other hands, especially as it was promised that the policy of the paper would not be changed, and Mr. Nye, although he had also sold his interest, was to remain as editor. The transfer took place in 1898. At first I hardly knew how to deport myself, after being so suddenly released from the numerous cares and duties that I had been methodically performing daily for years. I can not describe the sensation of relief. While in the business, every day and every moment of the hours when awake demanded my time in some form of thought or action, and nothing leisurely. Everything was done with the greatest speed, that all expected of me might be accomplished. Going on for over thirty years, this business practice had almost become a habit of life.

It was my privilege, as Superintendent of the mint, to participate in the administration of one of the most interesting eras of the coinage history of our country. In this was embraced the record of the greatest volume of gold coinage; the introduction of the Philippine coinage; the radical change in designs of our gold coins; the adoption of the new electrolytic method of refining, and the first introduction of improved machinery and methods in coinage operations. In short, these were the years of the greatest activity of the mints of the United States.

When I became Superintendent in 1897, the mint contained six steam engines, located in various parts of the building, to supply the power required to operate the machinery and appliances used in refining and coinage operations. Electricity for power purposes was not yet in general use; the practicability of long transmission lines at low cost had not been fully worked out. Even at the high cost of electric power of those days, I considered that it would be more economical to discard all the steam engines and adopt the plan of individual electric motors, so as to be able to apply power singly to the machines as they might be needed in coinage operations. My recommendation was accepted and approved by the authorities at Washington. I arranged to change from steam to electricity so that there was no interference with the operations of the mint whatever. The old style of coke and coal melting furnaces, which had been the form used ever since the government erected the first mint in 1793, were discarded and replaced with furnaces in which gas and crude oil were used for fuel. Modern water tube boilers, with fuel oil burners, replaced the old-fashioned tubular boilers of the power plant. Relating these facts calls to mind an interesting and rather amusing experience we had with some charcoal dealers not long after I became Superintendent. The mint was using about $250 worth of charcoal monthly. At the letting of annual contracts for supplies, a certain dealer in wood and coal was the successful bidder on the charcoal item at $11 per ton, which was about what the government had been paying for previous years' supplies. There were other bids, ranging from $15 to $16 per ton. As is usual in such cases, the contract was awarded to the lowest bidder, who offered to supply the coal for $11 per ton. The contractor gave a bond for the faithful performance of his agreement, and for about a month supplied the charcoal as ordered by the mint authorities, when he came to me and regretfully said that he would have to default on his contract and sacrifice the amount of his bond, otherwise the men who were controlling the charcoal business would ruin him. He said that he was able to get enough charcoal to fill his contract, independent of his opponents, but that they had enough influence to prevent wholesalers selling him wood and some kinds of coal. Upon inquiry I found that we were using charcoal almost exclusively to start the fires in the metal melting furnaces. Thereupon I told the contractor that he need not worry about his bond. The government would let the contract stand in force for the year, but would not call upon him to furnish any more charcoal, as in fact it would not use any more. The gratitude and appreciation of release from the unpleasant position in which he had been, and the saving of the bond were made manifest by the hearty shake of my hand. I ordered a cord of four-foot pine wood cut into six-inch lengths. At the mint, these blocks were split up into ordinary kindling, and the melters were told to use this kindling thereafter in place of the charcoal, and when laying their fires they would be permitted to soak the wood with coal oil, if necessary. Some of the old hands said it would be impossible to start the fires in that manner, but when asked why could only say, "It never has been done that way." However, upon the whole, the men entered into the spirit of the change and after the first morning discarded the use of coal oil, and as long as the coke and coal furnaces were in use in the mint the hands never used another lot of charcoal, and would not have used it as a matter of preference had there been a supply on hand. In the course of a month or more afterward the spokesman of the charcoal combine called on me and offered me a supply at a reduced figure, which of course I declined. He pointed out that the government could not get it from any other source. When I said that that might be so, he asked, why wouldn't we buy it from him. I replied, "Because we are done with using charcoal in the mint, especially when we can make $8 worth of pine answer the purpose of $250 worth of charcoal." The man was speechless. I never saw him again.

Some years before I became Superintendent, the depart-

In the Service of the Government

ment at Washington had directed that anthracite coal be used under the steam generating boilers, as this coal gave off no appreciable amount of smoke. The neighborhood had been making complaint of being annoyed by the smoke from the bituminous coals used. I knew of a lignite, remarkably free from smoke, mined in Oregon, which made an excellent fuel for steam boilers. I was able to have this coal laid down in the mint at about one-quarter of the cost of anthracite. Of course it required more pounds of the lignite to produce a given amount of steam than anthracite, yet the change netted the government a saving of over $700 per month in the cost of steam fuel. After the great development of oil wells in California, the cost of fuel was reduced to a still lower notch by the introduction of oil burners under the boilers and the use of oil as a fuel.

I think I found about as much interest in the operations of the refining department as anywhere else in the mint. With the discovery of the rich gold deposits on the Yukon River, bringing, as it did, a very great addition to the gold deposits at our institution, the importance of the refinery operations was correspondingly increased. The department was originally equipped with a plant for the nitric acid process. Subsequently a small sulphuric acid plant was added, when it was found that the process with the latter acid was more economical. When the gold deposits were so largely increased by the influx from the Far North, the old nitric plant was torn out to give place to the addition needed by the later-adopted process. All the wood work of the old plant was burned and the metal parts were melted, and from the ashes and meltings we recovered gold and silver of considerably greater value than the cost of the new addition to the refinery. Prior to this time, but little attention was given to saving the copper sulphate, which was a by-product in the operations of the refinery. A few crystallizing tanks had been provided, but the number was insufficient, and even then the solution was turned into the tanks only when the refinery hands could be spared for the purpose. At other times the solution of copper sulphate went down into the sewers. The idea was that the cost of crystallizing the solution would not be met by the returns from the sale of bluestone or copper sulphate. A complete system of tanks, pumps, and drying houses was installed, and all the solution was converted into bluestone and readily sold to consumers and dealers. Several thousand dollars per year were saved to the government by taking care of and marketing this by-product. The law required that the refineries of the mint should be operated as near to cost as possible, so that the cost of refining gold and silver, which is borne by the depositors, shall be reduced to the smallest possible figure without loss to the government. My predecessor had to deal with an extravagant organization when he took possession of the mint. The refinery had run behind in the previous four years and piled up a deficit of $82,230. He had made a decided improvement in conditions, but was unable, through the small volume of business, to place the refinery on a self-sustaining basis. However, his deficit for four years was only $15,361. In the first four years of my administration the earnings were $205,943, and cost of operation $206,205, a difference of only $262. Through the refinery having been operated at a loss for more than twenty years, there was a deficit of about $150,000. There was only one way to make this amount good, and that was to increase the earnings and reduce the cost of operations, which I did, so that before I resigned my position in 1907 the total deficit was wiped off the books by the annual credit of surplus earnings.

After the first six years of my administration as Superintendent, I had occasion to make an investigation of cost operation in the coinage department and wastage for that period. I found that in that time, we had handled $1,200,000,000 of gold. The law recognizes the difficulty in handling gold without some wastage, and fixes the limit of allowance of loss in melting at .001 per cent, and in coinage .0005 per cent; and our legal wastage with these limitations could have been $900,000 in the six years, whereas it was only $6361. In the matter of coinage and cost per piece turned out, the result also was gratifying to us all. Although the amount appropriated by Congress for coinage purposes for the San Francisco mint during the six years of my administration had been but little more than had been allowed for corresponding periods during three previous administrations, yet we had been able to produce nearly double the number of pieces of coin, or practically double the coinage. What was more satisfactory was that the cost per piece had been reduced from 4 cents and 6 mills to 1 cent and 6 mills, for the three years' work from 1902 to 1905.

The mint work was interesting from several standpoints, and not least were the metallurgical problems that frequently developed. They had to be worked out for the reason that there was little in technical books to direct us or to explain the difficulties. Our greatest troubles began when bullion from cyanide plants became common in deposits. At first the miners did not appreciate the necessity of freeing their product from zinc that became associated with the gold in the process of recovery, and its presence in the bullion not only made it difficult to determine accurately the value of the gold by assaying, but whenever any of the zinc or lead failed of elimination in the refining operation, there was trouble in the coining rooms when the operators there had to make the bullion into coin. It is remarkable how small a quantity of these impurities would make the gold unfit for coinage. As much as one part of lead or zinc to 999 of gold would render the metal absolutely unworkable in the coinage room. I have seen gold ingots, cast for the making of double eagles, or twenty-dollar pieces, so brittle from the presence of a small amount of these impurities that they would break in pieces when dropped on the stone floor of the rolling room. All problems of this character were eliminated when the electrolytic method of refining was substituted for the sulphuric acid process. The metal refined by electrolysis was converted to a practically pure state.

Not long after the cyanide process for gold recovery was in general use, a man came into the Superintendent's office and introduced himself as a miner and mine owner from the State of Nevada. He said he had a very private matter that he wanted to discuss with me, as he had been told that I could help him out of his difficulties. He first asked the privilege of shutting the office door so that his conversation could not be overheard by persons outside. Then he went on to say that he was sure that one of the largest and most responsible firms of bullion buyers in the city had been robbing him. He said that the bullion he had been shipping to this firm was a combination of gold and silver, with considerably greater quantity of silver than gold. The shipments were made about one per month, and until the last three months the returns from the buyers had been very satisfactory, agreeing with the mine manager's assay, but that during the last three months, there had been a decided falling off in the buyers' allowance for silver contents of his bullion. In reply to my inquiry, he said that the allowance for gold was all right. He also said that he had a very superior chemist in charge of his cyanide plant. When I asked the mining man how long this new and very "superior chemist" had been in his employ, he replied that he had secured him about three months before. His confidence in the "superior" ability of his new man was so great he had not noticed that the beginning of the period of his complaint of losses was about the time of the introduction of the new man in his works. In further response to my questions as to the details of operating his cyanide plant, he went on to tell me how the new man "soaked" the precipitates from the cyanide solution (which, of course, was the product of gold and silver from his ores) "in strong sulphuric acid for twenty-four hours," explaining that this final treatment of the bullion eliminated the zinc and other impurities that might be there. I then asked him what he did with the acid after it had been drawn off from the precious metals, or after he was through with the "soaking" process. "Oh," said he, "we throw it away!" I explained to him that the silver in the finely divided state was almost as soluble in the acid as the zinc, so that his "very superior chemist" had been throwing away a good part of his silver with the acid, and thus, in all probability, his suspicion of wrong doing on the part of the bullion buyers was unwarranted. He was dazed for a moment, and when he recovered his speech said that he "didn't see how his man could make such a blunder, as he was a thorough chemist, having worked in a drug store all his life!" He thanked me, but I never saw him again. However, I think there was a "superior chemist" who lost his job on short notice.

A very strange and interesting feature in relation to volatilization of precious metal arose while I was investigating the extent of furnace losses in the metal process of the coinage operations. I discovered one day that gold and silver in a finely divided state, but in globular form, were being deposited on the floor of the mint court, which is in the center of the building. A sweeping of the roof and gutters of the building gave a very good return in gold and silver. Such of the furnaces as were not equipped with dust and vapor-arresting chambers I immediately had rebuilt, adding the gold and silver saving device. The first year's saving more than paid for the expense. Upon looking into the subject further I found that the metals, when condensed from the vapor form, assumed the shape of perfect globules. In this case they were so minute that it required the use of a microscope to see them. I found precious metals inside the melting rooms, on all wall or other projections that would hold dust, as well as in adjacent rooms, in addition to that found in the court and on the roof. While there might be some question as to the form in which the gold was drawn up through the furnace chimneys and deposited in minute spheres on the roof and court of the building, there seems little room for argument that the metal was projected from the melting pots thirty feet or more across the room to find lodgment on the walls in the form of these minute globules, while other globules were being drawn up the chimneys as solids. A force strong enough to overcome the draft of the chimneys would have sent the globules with such force that the working men standing between the melting pots and walls, seemingly would have been struck by some of the little pellets of gold and silver if in solid form while in movement. No such sensation was ever experienced nor did we find any evidence of the metals leaving the furnace in solid form. The best explanation I have heard is that the metal in gaseous or vapor form, soon after its release from the heat which vaporized it, first returned to liquid form, in which, by surface contraction, it would be forced into globular form, when the cool atmosphere would quickly solidify it, returning it by the same steps through a cooling atmosphere, from gas to a solid, as by which, through heat, it passed from a solid to gas.

T. A. Rickard, the talented editor of the *Mining and Scientific Press* of San Francisco, asked me if I knew why some gold coins fresh from the mint possessed a slight greenish tinge. I had some experiments made to determine the cause, and found that a decided green color

In the Service of the Government

could be given to gold by adding silver in certain proportions to it. We knew that the presence of silver in gold bullion influenced the shades of its color, and the presence of copper had the same effect, and naturally attributed a green shade to the copper; but to our great surprise, after experiments in making many different combinations of pure gold, silver, and copper, we were unable to develop any bullion of a decided green color until we entirely eliminated the copper and melted together 700 parts of gold with 300 parts of silver. This combination gave a decidedly light shade of green. We obtained a decidedly darker shade of green by combining 900 parts of gold with only 100 parts of silver. To account for the green appearance of some gold coin it must be explained that the regulations allowed the presence of ten parts of silver out of 1000 parts of gold bullion to remain with the gold that was prepared for coinage, it being impractical, with the refining processes in use in those days, to remove all the silver from the crude bullion. It was always taken into account, when adding the copper for alloy, that of silver and copper there should not be more than the 10 per cent fixed by law. The blanks or disks cut for coins, before being stamped or pressed, were annealed, which is a process that requires heating the blanks up to a cherry red. This caused the particles of copper in the surface of the blanks to form the black oxide of copper. As the oxide is quite soluble, the subsequent dropping of the blanks that had been heated into a bath of diluted acid removed all the copper from the surface of the blanks, leaving in place a film of gold combined with what silver was left in the metal by the refiners, which frequently came near amounting to 1 per cent, and sufficient, under the procedure described, to impart a greenish shade to the coins. Why a white metal combined with a yellow metal should produce a green color I was unable to explain, a determination of the matter being beyond our equipment for investigation. The experiences mentioned are samples of the many we had, and are given to illustrate the character of problems and matters with which we had to deal.

Altogether, I suppose I had the most varied, exciting, and interesting, as well as distracting experiences of any other mint Superintendent that was ever commissioned in the United States. I have not attempted to relate all the incidents pertaining to my administration, especially some of the unpleasant matters involving acts of dishonest employees. The facts are matter of record, the offending parties in most cases were punished and are now trying to earn an honest living, and I would not say a word or write a line that would hinder or embarrass them in their praiseworthy efforts. Under the law that makes the Superintendent responsible for all losses of every character, my bondsmen had to make good to the government the theft of $30,000 in 1900, and in turn I had to deed over to the bonding company my real estate in Oakland which included the old homestead. I wanted the company to take some valuable mining property instead of the home place, but the company was afraid of mines and insisted on taking the Oakland property. However, this apparent misfortune was not a lasting one. A relief bill was introduced in Congress which had the indorsement of the Secretary of the Treasury and Director of the Mint, and the active support of Senator Perkins and Congressman Knowland. Much to my surprise and gratification, the measure was passed by both houses in the session of its introduction and was promptly signed by the President. It was the first time that a bill of this character, relating to a Pacific Coast beneficiary, was made a law in so short a time. Usually Congress takes from ten to fifteen years, or more, for consideration of acts of this kind of relief. It was due to the earnest work and influence of Senator Perkins and Congressman Knowland that an exception was made in this case. The appropriation enabled me to repay the surety company and receive deeds for the return of the property I had turned over to it a few months before. It was in connection with the loss of the $30,000 and the ferreting out of the party responsible for it that I became acquainted with William J. Burns, now of international reputation as the greatest of detectives. The friendship begun then has continued until this day. I should have said that he gave no small aid in the passage by Congress of the relief bill in my interest, when mentioning those to whom I was especially indebted for the enactment of that measure. I saw much of Mr. Burns in after years when he was prosecuting the Oregon land fraud cases for the government, and was able to render him some assistance in the famous San Francisco graft cases. When the scene of his activities was transferred to the Atlantic states and his business called him at times to San Francisco, he never failed to pay me a visit. Mr. Burns is a man of fine personality, polished, and an intensely interesting conversationalist; a man of high ideals, and incorruptible; he is endowed with a power of insight into human nature, an intuition, and a judgment of the acts of men that are something wonderful. These qualities, coupled with his utter lack of fear and a tenacity of purpose without limit, are the broad basis on which his great reputation rests.

In 1905 Mr. Burns gave me considerable assistance in a matter of investigation which I had been directed by the department to make. This was in the United States assay office at Seattle, where there existed some evidence of wrong doing on the part of some one connected with the institution. The case turned out to be one of very great importance, and the incidents involved gave it a character of unusual interest. At this time most of the deposits of gold made at the assay office were in the form of gold dust, nearly all of which came from the mines in Alaska. Gold in this form always carries a small per cent of black sand, which the miners can not eliminate from the gold dust without washing out the little fine particles of gold associated with it. When the gold dust is melted into bars by the government, or any one, for that matter, the sand goes off with the flux, and of course the gold, after melting, will weigh less than gold dust before melting, to the extent of the said elimination. I had made quite a study in our work at the mint of these apparent losses, and had found that the average loss should not exceed 5 per cent. So when complaint reached the Washington authorities from depositors at the Seattle assay office that they were suffering greater losses than they thought they should, I was directed to make an investigation of the matter. I was quite certain that something was wrong there. I took with me to assist in the work on this errand Lee Kerfoot, an exceedingly bright young employee of the mint. He was a graduate of the University of California, with experience in the melting of gold and dealing with the metallurgical problems arising from the work. My first step was to look over the institution and find out how the place was conducted, expecting to find the leak where there was laxity in adherence to the regulations. I found the office part of the work seemingly carried on with excellent system, and with every regard for the regulations and check required, but in the melting rooms, so far as proper supervision and care against dishonest losses were concerned, things were loosely conducted. For this reason I began the investigation in this department. Mr. Burns had assigned two first-class men to assist me, whom I detailed to run down the habits, past and present, of all employees of the melting room. This required about two weeks' work. In the meantime, Mr. Kerfoot and I were making experiments and taking notes of the daily operations in the melting room as if we expected to find the cause of the undue losses accountable to unskilfulness and carelessness in the melting operations. I personally took the weight of each deposit as it went to the melting room, and there every handling was closely watched by Mr. Kerfoot, until the deposit after melting came back and was weighed by me, and the losses in melting noted. Notwithstanding this care and watchfulness, at the end of each day's work the sum of the losses exceeded what experience told us should occur. It was plain that the stealing was still being practiced, notwithstanding our presence. The realization of this fact made us feel as if the fellow who was guilty of the dishonest work thought he was so shrewd and had his tracks so well covered that he could safely continue his stealing during our presence there, and was practically laughing in our faces. It was as if we were challenged to a contest in which the unknown was putting his skill and shrewdness against our wit. The thought, no doubt, acted as a spur in our determination to locate the thief. The reports of the detectives failed to show anything that would indicate that the workmen investigated were leading any other than normal lives. In fact, their characters and habits proved to be beyond criticism. Two weeks or more had passed without having discovered the slightest clue, and I was becoming discouraged, for in whatever direction we prodded it was without result, and the losses were going on daily with a regularity that was hard to accept as caused by dishonesty. One morning, while contemplating the situation and mentally going over all the procedures in receiving, melting, and depositing of the bullion that was being tampered with, I was reminded that all the deposits that came in the afternoon did not come direct to me to be sent out to the melting room, but were taken in charge by the cashier, and by him placed in the vault over night and then given to the melters in the morning. Instantly I felt that the path leading to a solution of the matter had been discovered.

I am sure that if any one had noticed me at that moment I would have betrayed the excited state of my mind. I immediately went to the books and made calculations of the losses on the morning deposit receipts that went direct to the melting room, and, as I expected, found the losses normal, and when I figured the losses on the afternoon deposit receipts that were taken in charge by the cashier and put in the vault over night I found them to run about 3 per cent greater than they should. I had been looking for the trouble in the wrong department. Here was a trail leading in another direction. It was not only a plain trail, but I could make out the man who had made it—none other than the cashier. Through little inquiry, I found out that the cashier was in the habit of coming down to the office a half hour or more before the time of beginning work and opening up the office, for the purpose, he said, of getting out the deposits kept in the vault over night so that the melters would not be delayed in starting their labors for the day. I knew then that he used this time to rob the deposits, and to do this without detection he had to make a substitution of black sand in weight for the gold removed. During the cashier's absence to lunch, I managed to get access to the vault and found the balances, or scales, in a tin box, which were necessary to weigh the gold in making the substitution. It was imperative for the success of his scheme that the deposits should weigh exactly the same, when he turned them over to the head melter, as when they were received the day before by the receiving clerk. We soon found that he used a dark-colored sand to replace the gold he took from the deposits, and Mr. Kerfoot, by some exceedingly clever work, found that the cashier obtained the sand from some distance at a point on Puget Sound shores. It was obtained under an assumed name in quite large quantities. He had used altogether in the dishonest work over a quarter of a ton of sand.

Although we were now positive of the guilt of the cashier, some evidence stronger than any we had was necessary before he could be charged with the crime. Therefore, we arranged with the manager of the bank which had filed the complaint at Washington that caused the investigation to supply us with a lot of gold dust, from which we sifted every particle of sand, and even all the small particles of gold. This was sealed in the presence of witnesses and sent to the assay office during an afternoon by a messenger, with a witness. It was noted by proper witnesses that the deposit was subsequently taken in charge by the cashier and placed in the vault. The next morning, when the deposit was turned over to the melter, instead of allowing it to go to the melting pot, we sifted it and recovered about *three ounces of sand*. As the deposit had not been increased in weight after its receipt, it was plain that an amount of gold equal to the weight of said sand had been abstracted. As we had been sifting deposits and manipulating them in various ways, our treatment of this particular deposit had no particular significance with the workmen who saw us working with it. Nevertheless, the cashier, within two or three days afterward, came down to the office in the morning, and instead of applying himself wholly to his work, busied himself with other matters. Among other things, he went to the vault and brought out the tin box which I was sure contained the balances with which he made his weights in the substitution process. Becoming convinced that he was preparing for flight, Mr. Kerfoot, who was on watch at the assay office for any such action during my absence, gave the signal to the secret service men who were conveniently posted outside, for the arrest of the cashier. He professed surprise and amusement that he should be charged with any wrong doing. He was taken to the office of the secret service men and was told with what offense he was charged. He was directed to open the tin box. He hesitated. When further commanded, he held the key to the lock, again hesitating, as if to delay the exposure of positive incriminating evidence. The secret service officer again spoke, demanding compliance with his request. The cashier obeyed, and with the raising of the lid of the box exposed to view a neat pair of balances with numerous little grains of gold dust scattered around on the bottom of the box, plainly showing the use the scales had been put to. The incident was further heightened by the cashier crumpling up and falling to the floor as if in a faint. After he "came to," or became composed, he confessed to some slight peculation, but denied responsibility for all the losses that had been going on for five years past. On his person the officers found $12,000 in currency that he had drawn from the bank that morning, leaving $3000 to his credit in his account, as we subsequently found when searching the city for property and money in his name. The sum of these two items represented a good part of his thefts for that year. This bank was a new institution, and he represented to the official that he was interested in or owned some good mines in Alaska, and that he desired to deposit his gold with the bank and have the bank dispose of it and credit him with the proceeds, as he, being an employee of the assay office, was prohibited from selling or depositing gold there. He stored up his daily stealings, and on days corresponding with the arrivals of steamers from Alaska would appear at the bank with a bag of gold dust and leave it there to be disposed of in accordance with the arrangements just mentioned. In that way he had acquired the credit of $15,000.

Knowing now how the cashier had been feloniously operating, it was incumbent upon us to discover to what extent his stealing operations had reached. This necessitated taking account of every deposit made in the assay office in the afternoons for that year and the preceding

In the Service of the Government

four years, and computing the difference between a normal loss and the loss shown by the books, which would approximately represent the stealings. This was not only a tedious but a complicated job, for the normal loss on gold varied with the districts from whence it came. Here again was where my young friend Kerfoot's talents came into play and rendered service hard to duplicate. By these computations we found the total of stealings to reach an amount somewhere near $150,000. I do not recall the exact figures. The next thing for us to do was to find where he sold the gold and what he did with the proceeds. It took some time, but we succeeded in locating his sales, which had been made once a year or thereabouts, and were pleased to find that the amounts of gold sold agreed exceedingly close with the amounts estimated by us to have been stolen. We had great trouble in finding out what he did with the gold stolen in the years of 1903 and 1904.

After exhausting the possibilities of the cashier having disposed of his stolen gold in Seattle in 1903, we knew that he must have taken it to some other place. But where? The attendance record at the assay office showed that at no time was there more than two consecutive days when he did not record himself as having been at the office. We then made a search in those cities which he might have visited by taking no more than two days' time for such a trip, but found nothing to indicate he had ever visited any of the places. The cashier himself explained those two days' absence by saying that he had spent them in a visit to friends in Portland, but we could not verify even that. We were well nigh discouraged when it occurred to us that the two days might have been Monday and Tuesday, which would have enabled him to use Sunday in traveling, making three days, and if he left the office Saturday morning, after recording his presence, and then returning late Wednesday afternoon in time to record his presence, he would have practically five days, which was the exact time it would have taken to go to San Francisco and back, arriving there in the morning and taking the train back in the evening. I immediately went to San Francisco and called on the officials of the Selby Smelting and Lead Company, explaining the case to them and telling them that I was sure that the cashier had, on the 18th day of November, 1903, sold to their firm about $16,000 worth of gold dust. An examination of the books showed that a purchase of just about that much had been made on that date. The receiving clerk was asked if there was anything about the man's action that would cause him to remember the appearance of the person who sold the gold to the firm. He promptly replied in the affirmative. He stated that, in the first place, the man declared that he was on his way East and must have his money that day, and insisted on paying a discount for the favor of getting the money at once, instead of waiting twenty-four hours, as was the rule for making payments. Then, again, he refused a check or coin, and would take nothing but currency. It is the practice at this institution to give a man a receipt for his bullion, which he holds while the gold is being assayed and its value ascertained, and which is surrendered upon being paid. The receipt in this transaction was issued to a name different from that of the guilty cashier, but the indorsement was plainly in his handwriting, and he had made some figures on the back of the receipt, computing the loss in melting, which were unmistakably his. Moreover, the clerk's description of the man closely tallied with the general appearance of the cashier. I was certain now that we had located the stealings and verified the amount for the year 1903. However, I wanted to make the evidence stronger. I felt satisfied that he would not dare to purchase a return railroad ticket and travel under an assumed name, as he would be likely to meet trainmen and other people who knew him, so I

In the Service of the Government

went to the railroad office and found that a ticket to Seattle had been sold on November 18 to the cashier in his proper name. The stub of this ticket, with the cashier's signature, was given me to be used in the trial. The evidence in this transaction was now complete, but we had yet to locate the sale made in 1904. This was a more difficult task, as his movements for the year had been more varied, and besides he was married early in December and had gone East on his wedding trip. We first concluded that it was on this trip he disposed of an accumulation of stealings of about 1000 ounces, valued at between $16,000 and $17,000. We thought that he would find some way to dispose of it at the United States assay office in New York, and that he would put himself to some trouble to accomplish it. We felt that he would undoubtedly make the deposit through a third party, and by his knowledge of the government's method of doing business, he would feel protected from robbery by any middleman or messenger. We endeavored to have the officials at the assay office assist us in locating the sale there, but through some misunderstanding or error in description the officials reported that no purchase of that magnitude in gold dust had been made by them that season. The findings of the officials threw us off the right track and in consequence of the blunder we spent weeks in inquiries and searched through each city where the cashier and his bride stopped on the roundabout way from Seattle to New York, requiring investigations in San Francisco, Los Angeles, St. Louis, Pittsburgh, and New York City. In reviewing all this work it did not seem to us that any possibility had been overlooked. Nevertheless, we made another very careful search through San Francisco, but not a clue was found. I then began to think the officials at the government assay office at New York might have made a mistake. Finally I became positive in my mind that they had overlooked the deposit. I then wired the

Director of the Mint to cause another examination of the books of the New York institution, expressing my belief that on or about December 13 or 14 they would surely find a record of a deposit of gold dust of about 1000 ounces. The Director kindly took up the matter and I had the gratification of soon receiving a telegram in return saying that such a deposit as I had described had been made. It did not take long to connect the cashier with the transaction and secure evidence proving that he was the depositor. He sent the gold to the government office through the aid of a messenger, and all the communication he had with the office was over a telephone, located at a hotel other than that at which he was registered. The signatures made by him on the documents issued in the transactions were easily identified as being in the handwriting of the guilty cashier, although he used a fictitious name. Other facts were developed which helped to complete the chain of evidence of the man's guilt. The locating of this deposit also completed accounting for the amount estimated by us to have been stolen during the five years of his dishonest operations. We had been short in finding the disposition of all of his stealings for the last year, and finally reached the conclusion that in all probability he had not sold it and the gold would be found secreted somewhere around his home. Mr. Kerfoot, with the assistance of a secret service officer, went to the home of the cashier, and together they made a most thorough search of the premises, including the residence, garage, and other outbuildings and grounds. They had been at work several hours and had found where the cashier had endeavored to hide some black sand which was of the lot he had been using in making substitution for the stolen gold, as well as some of the appliances he had used in the dishonest work, when a setter dog belonging to the cashier brought in his mouth and laid down at the feet of the searchers a small buckskin pouch, as if

In the Service of the Government

he, too, had joined in the hunt for evidence against his master. The pouch still contained a few grains of gold, showing the use that had been made of it. However, so far, the gold the officers were in search of had not been discovered, although they had searched and poked into every nook, cranny, and corner from the roof to the basement of the residence, and were now in the cellar and about to give up the search, when Mr. Kerfoot called attention to the pile of about three tons of coal in a corner of the basement that they had not moved, although they had moved and repiled a cord or two of stove wood, and remarked that, to make the job complete, they would have to shovel it across the basement, so the two men started in on the job. They joked each other about being coal-heavers, especially when their complexions began to take on the hue of blackness that follows that vocation. They little expected that in the last possible place to be searched and under the last shovelful of coal to be moved in the remotest corner of the coal bin they would find two fat buckskin pouches containing the amount of gold missing from the estimate of the year's stealings, about $7000, but such was their reward.

In relating the story of this crime, I have only touched on some of the main and interesting features. The cashier pleaded guilty to stealing the gold missing for the year 1905. He was not charged and tried with the crimes committed in the other years, on the motion of the Assistant United States Attorney. He was sentenced to ten years' imprisonment.

The government seized all the property that could be found standing in his name, except the homestead and one or two other smaller pieces of real estate. The cashier was not extravagant and had not wasted the stealings. On the contrary, he had invested the proceeds of his rascally work with excellent judgment, largely in "near in" real estate, which had enhanced in value to a considerable extent. He accounted to his friends for these purchases by stories of rich relatives dying from time to time and leaving him large sums of money. The government sold the property and with the proceeds endeavored to restore to the miners the amounts of their losses. Considerable publicity was given of the intention of the government in the matter, but less than 50 per cent of the total amount stolen by the cashier was awarded to those who filed claims in the case. He had a number of influential friends who worked incessantly for a pardon and finally succeeded in getting him released from prison after he had served about six or seven years of the term of his sentence. He returned to Seattle and these friends found a good position for him, but in less than ninety days he was arrested once more and in prison. This time it was on a charge of taking some part in making counterfeit money. He was tried and convicted and sent back to the government prison.

He came from a good family, was refined in appearance, was bright, and had pleasant mannerisms, which made him well liked, if not popular. His was a strange case.

Chapter 2

Great Earthquake and Fire of 1906

PERHAPS I should class my experience in the great fire and earthquake of April, 1906, as the most exciting feature of my administration as Superintendent of the mint in San Francisco. While I would not seek another such experience, I have often said that I was glad the opportunity fell to me to be present and in the midst of one of the great disasters of history, but I shall always censure myself that I did not make a record of what I saw, as well as the observations of other people and my own thoughts while the circumstances and details of the awful affair were fresh in my mind. I was suddenly awakened soon after 5 o'clock on that memorable morning of April 18, with the hundreds of thousands of others who lived within a radius of a hundred miles of this section, to a realization of being shaken by an earthquake that seemed to threaten to tear our house to pieces. The building danced a lively jig, jumping up and down a good part of a foot at every jump, at the same time swaying this way and that; the walls and ceilings were twisting and squirming, as if wrestling to tear themselves asunder or one to throw the other down. Then there were the terrifying noises, the cracking and creaking of timber, the smashing and crashing of falling glass, bric-a-brac, and furniture, and the thumping of falling bricks coursing down the roof sides from the chimney tops. Now and then there would be a louder crash and roar, coming from some distance, that told, plainer than words, of the awfulness of the visitation and the greater destruction of property, if not life. The air was filled with dust. It seemed as if the shaking would never cease. Every vibration seemed to be followed by another more fierce, stronger, and more destructive. I lay in bed and saw the debris of wrecked chimney tops go sailing down past our bedroom windows. I felt that I was in as safe a place there as anywhere else in the house while the shaking lasted, and much safer than to attempt to go out of doors. Then I also felt that if the terrible disturbance was primary to the end of all things we might as well meet our fate right where we were. I confess that for a few seconds I was impressed with the idea that the end of the world had been reached. I did not get out of bed until the shaking ceased. Hastily dressing, I hurried to the street, expecting to find many houses wrecked and churches and other large buildings in ruins. I was greatly surprised to find so little damage done. A church tower had tumbled down on Telegraph Avenue a couple of blocks from our house, and its debris practically blockaded the street. A frame building, an old two-story rickety affair, at the intersection of Hobart Street and Broadway, had fallen flat. A larger, built-over frame apartment house on Eleventh Street was wrecked so it had to be taken down. Nearly every brick building in town suffered a loss of fire walls, while three or four old buildings were so badly injured that they were subsequently removed and new buildings erected in their place. The modern steel-framed structures went through the test without serious injury. The tall buildings were as immune from injury as the smaller ones. There was not a building in Oakland, Alameda, or Berkeley, that I heard of, that was not shorn of its chimney tops. This contributed no small amount of discomfort in household affairs, especially in culinary operations. People who relied upon gas stoves for their kitchen needs were not discommoded any length of time. On this side of the bay the gas and water mains did not suffer any serious damage. There was not a household that did not suffer some loss from broken crockery, ornaments, furniture, etc. Interiors, in some instances, were flooded by the breaking of water pipes inside of the houses. The addition of soot, broken plaster, and the liquid contents of broken glass containers increased the misery in many homes.

People who were on the street during the earthquake said that the shaking of the houses made a terrific din. The houses, and especially the roofs, emitted clouds of dust. Tree tops and telegraph poles were swaying several feet back and forth, and the surface of the streets running east and west moved in undulations not unlike the waves on the bay. With all of the tumbling of chimneys, crumbling of fire walls, and falling buildings, only two or three people were killed in Oakland, and not more than a score of injuries were reported. People were frightened and many could not be induced to enter their homes for a length of time—some for hours and some for days. Fortunately, we were having a spell of about as fine weather as one could wish for. The air was warm and balmy for a couple of days more, so it was no hardship to eat and to sleep out of doors, as many people did, until driven in by the cold winds and rain storm a little later on. Our family ate their breakfast inside the house, though it was cooked out in the back yard on a camp fire. People who had gas stoves were soon able to resume their cooking operations in the house, the gas company having quickly repaired damages to its plant and renewed the supply of gas. But people who depended on wood or coal stoves, with chimneys to carry off the smoke, were not allowed to use them until the chimneys were examined by a city inspector, who would then issue a permit. Bricklayers were in great demand for several weeks.

After an early breakfast, and finding that none of our family had been hurt, I walked down town to see what had happened and hear what I might from other places. Upon reaching Fourteenth and Broadway my thoughts for the first time touched upon San Francisco, and I instinctively turned my eyes in its direction. I saw that the heavens above the city were filling with the black smoke of a great fire, which was rapidly finishing the work of destruction begun by the earthquake, and that a disaster more appalling than anything ever dreamed of and more extensive in destruction of property ever before known was now upon the unfortunate city. Under the circumstances I knew my presence was needed, or at least my place of duty was at the mint, to direct and assist in protecting the government property placed under my care as Superintendent. I had great difficulty in making the trip to the city. The local trains connecting with the ferry-boats were not running on schedule, and when a train did come along the roofs and platforms were covered with people who could not get inside. It seemed as if about all of Oakland's population was bound for San Francisco, but few people, however, were carried over by the ferry-boats. The trains were halted along the line between Broadway and the pier. By riding on one until it stopped, then running ahead and getting aboard of another and walking from the foot of Seventh Street to the end of the pier, I finally reached the ferry slip, to be told that no one was allowed to go on the boats bound for the city and that the boats would only be run to bring refugees from San Francisco. I hunted up Mr. Palmer, the division superintendent, and asked him to make an exception of my case and let me go over. He said he fully appreciated the circumstances of my request and would send me across the bay immediately. I was directed to go aboard one of the ferry-boats in the slip and was soon on the way to the city that was being ravaged by fires arising in almost every direction. I took a position on the upper deck as far forward as possible and tried to pick out the districts threatened by the flames. At this hour there were several distinct and separate conflagrations, which merged into one great, sweeping fire later in the day. The fires were started, no doubt, by the disturbance of electric wires, upsetting of stoves, etc., in half a dozen or more sections of the city, but more particularly in the wholesale district, the water front section, and the district through to the Mission from the bay. The earthquake had broken the water pipes in the streets in many places, therefore the mains were empty and no water was to be had by the firemen at any of the hydrants. They were helpless away from the water front. By getting water from the bay, the fire department prevented the flames from spreading to the docks and warehouses on the piers, and also saved considerable other property adjacent to the waterfront.

It was a terrible sight. Flames were leaping high in the air from places scattered all the way across the front part of the city. Great clouds of black smoke filled the sky and hid the rays of the sun. Buildings in the track of the rapidly spreading fire went down like houses of cardboard; little puffs of smoke would issue from every crevice for a brief time, to be suddenly followed by big clouds of black smoke which would hide things for an instant, as if in attempt to shut out the vision of the tragedy being enacted. Great masses of flame would quickly take the place of the smoke and shoot up above everything, announcing the consummation of destruction, and then sweep on to the doomed one next in order. I could see that the devastation was going on in the very midst of the most important and costly part of the city—the wholesale, financial, and retail districts. How far the fire had extended I could not make out; whether the mint structure had yet been subjected to the fury of the flames I could not determine. The uncertainty increased my anxiety to reach the building.

Landing from the ferry, I found both sides of Market Street for several blocks from the ferry building to be in a mass of flames. Passage up town was also blocked by the flames by the way of Mission, Howard, Folsom, and other parallel streets on the south. To the north, along the water front, I made my way on docks, passing in front of the burning buildings facing the bay, amid firemen fighting the flames, and hundreds of refugees racing for the ferry building, having learned that the cities of Oakland, Alameda, and Berkeley afforded an asylum for the homeless of San Francisco. These people were of all classes and conditions, young and old, male and female. Many were laden with all they could carry of household things, pet animals, and birds in their cages, but more people passed along in the race for a safer place with no loads or packages to hinder them. By use of the word "race" I do not mean to imply that the movements of the crowds indicated any showing of panic. On the contrary, I did not see a single person in tears or manifesting fear. Every one seemed to realize that all were menaced by the same danger and victims of the same misfortune, and were reduced to a common level for the time, at least—a condition which seemed to arouse the utmost confidence in one another. The sight of so much distress drove into obscurity the baser soul, to give the fullest play to all that was noble and good in man. Never was human life and person, or personal property so safe from injury or loss by depredation in San Francisco as on that terrible day, and for the several days following.

I went as far north as Jackson or Pacific Street, thence west around the fire. I found at Sansome Street the fire fighters concentrating their efforts there to prevent the fire from crossing the thoroughfare and spreading west; and as on Market Street, from the intersection of Sansome Street west as far as the street was built up, the fire had not been able to cross, it was thought and hoped that all that valuable property and business west of Sansome and north of Market were going to be saved from the conflagration. This hope remained strong until late in the afternoon, when the fire, slowly eating its way north on the east side of Sansome Street, reached a tall building between Clay and Washington streets which was filled, from cellar to attic, with inflammable goods. This structure made a terrific blaze, which was communicated to some frame buildings across the street which were very flimsy. The appellation, "fire fiend," seemed to be the only term appropriate at this point. The flames acted as if they knew that, so far, they had been prevented from crossing to the buildings on the other side all along Sansome Street, but now they had conquered the resistance after an all-day fight and hesitated only long enough to gather strength for a terrific and terrifying demonstration of their destructive powers. The buildings at the point of the crossing were wiped out in a few moments, then from a direction west across the territory thought to have been saved from the fire raced a column of flame about a block wide like a prairie fire, leaving the property bordering its path for more deliberate destruction. In almost less time than it takes to tell about it the flames jumped from Sansome to Montgomery, then from the latter street to Kearny, seizing upon Chinatown with a fury that terrified the poor Chinamen and prevented them from saving much or anything in the way of goods or personal effects. The fire moved more slowly in spreading in the other directions, but it was this particular part of the conflagration that completed the destruction of the business district and hotel section and burned for more than two days afterward before it was conquered by the firemen, citizens, and soldiers who, when routed at Sansome Street, retreated to Van Ness Avenue, and there put up a successful line of defense. The fire burned up to that street, but there it was stayed. The part of the conflagration which swept from the ferry building on through the wholesale district and thence through the Mission finally worked its way across Market Street and joined the Sansome Street branch of the fire. It would take too much space to attempt to relate all the details of the burning of the city. But in those three days of horror every bank, every theater, every newspaper, all the large business houses, and the homes of over one-third of the population of the city had been swept out of existence.

To return to the description of my efforts to reach the mint building: when I reached Kearny Street and found that I was out of the fire zone, I started in the direction of the mint, using Kearny, Sutter, and Post streets until I reached Union Square. In crossing Union Square I saw the dead body of a man wrapped in a quilt lying near the base of the Dewey monument. I was told that the unfortunate was a victim of the earthquake. I had now passed through a good portion of the substantial part of the city not yet attacked by the flames and was able to observe the damage caused by the earthquake. I was surprised to find that all the first-class buildings on good foundations were practically uninjured. There were some poorly constructed buildings erected on made ground which were thrown down, among which the hotel on Valencia Street, where the greatest loss of life took place, was a notable instance. Frame houses on solid ground but a short distance away on either side of the hotel showed little evidence of having passed through an earthquake.

After leaving Union Square I walked down Powell toward Market. Upon reaching the last named street I was stopped by the soldiers posted along the thorough-

A PHOTOGRAPH taken on the morning of the first day of the great fire that describes more vividly the extent and frightful character of the disaster than can be given in words. All the buildings in the foreground were destroyed within a few hours after the picture was taken.

fare to keep all people from passing into the burning district. Just what advantage to the public, property owners, or any one, for that matter, such use of the soldiers was, or of what value their instructions were, I could never learn or understand. The action of the troops prevented proprietors of stores and office people from visiting their places of business, securing papers, and saving personal belongings. They prevented the looting of the doomed stores, it is true, but probably it would have been better to have thrown the store doors open and let people carry off what they could than stand over the property with loaded rifles, threatening death to any who attempted to enter until the flames came along and devoured the stuff and relieved the soldiers. However, I was displeased with the manner in which the soldiers pushed me back, in my several attempts to cross Market Street at different points. Finally, at the intersection of Mason and Market streets, while trying to convince a guard that I was a government officer and that my duty called me across the street, a policeman who happened to know me came along, and finding out what I wanted ignored the soldier and escorted me to the other side of Market Street, thence down to Fifth Street, where the mint was located. I felt exceedingly grateful for his kindness and could not help admiring this evidence of superior judgment of the police over the military in this particular case.

When I reached the mint building I found that I had also reached the edge of the fire zone. A lot of small buildings directly opposite the mint building on Fifth Street had already been destroyed by the flames, and the fire was slowly eating its way northerly toward the Metropolitan Temple and Lincoln school building, both of which faced on Fifth Street; besides, from the center of the same block it was working its way more rapidly toward the big Emporium Building. Another branch of the flames had swept the buildings on the south side of Mission opposite the mint building, and was crossing Mission, heading for Market Street, clearly pointing out for destruction all the big buildings west and north of the mint; and it was also evident that before the afternoon was over the two fires would come together on Fifth Street, and thus cut off the mint building from communication with the outside world and surround it with fire, if not destroy it. Early in the beginning of the conflagration a great many of the poor people living in the vicinity of the mint brought quantities of bedding and other household things such as could be easily handled and piled the stuff on the walks around the building, thinking it would be safe there.

One of the initial fires, that finally merged with others in making the general conflagration, started a block below the mint on Fifth Street in a rickety frame building used as a boarding house. It was partially thrown down by the force of the earthquake shocks. A stove in which a fire had been started to cook breakfast was upset and the red-hot coals, when spilled out, set fire to the place. Firemen quickly appeared on the scene while the flames were yet small and could easily have been extinguished if any water could have been obtained from the hydrants. They could only stand by and watch the fire grow into an uncontrollable demon of blaze.

Inside the mint building I was greatly pleased to find fifty of our employees, whose sense of loyalty to duty had not been modified by fear of earthquake or the horror of being penned up in a big building surrounded by fire. They were there to do their best to help save the property of the government, and they went about the work in a simple, every-day manner, but nevertheless with earnest, willing, and active spirit. I felt proud to be Superintendent of that band of faithful and brave men. The captain of the watch, T. W. Hawes, had directed the work with excellent judgment until I arrived. They had fought the fire away from getting a foothold in the building from the east and south sides, but we all knew the worst was to come when the flames reached the big buildings to the west and north of us.

I made a trip over the inside of the building and had things made snug and had all inflammable material removed from proximity to the openings in the walls on the north and west sides. A survey from the roof about 1 o'clock in the afternoon made our position look rather perilous. It did not seem probable that the structure could withstand that terrific mass of flames that was sweeping down upon us from Market Street. The fire that had cut across Mission Street to the west of us had swept out northwesterly to Market Street, then east as if to join hands with the other branch of the fire then raging in and on both sides of the big Emporium Building; it had thus marshaled the elements of destruction and was now marching them down on the mint building. The battle would soon be on. Lieutenant Armstrong of the United States army was thoughtful enough to bring a squad of ten soldiers from Fort Miley to help in any way the men could be of service to us. These with our own men made a fighting crew of sixty, which was divided up into squads for work on each floor, from the basement to the roof. Fortunately for us, we had a good supply of water. In fact, it is a matter of interest to know that, some months previous, the suggestion came to me that we should have the building piped and fire hydrants and hose at suitable places installed on each floor to protect the building from any fire originating on the inside. It was only about ten days before the great disaster came upon us that the last hydrants of the system were put in place on the roof. Our water supply was independent of outside sources, being derived from an artesian well in the court. With a strong pump in the boiler room we were able to force a good stream to any part of the roof. Then the two large tanks located on the roof, filled with water, gave us a strong head for two hose streams at the basement floor. Without this protection the building would, without question, have been gutted by the flames. But even these alone would not have been sufficient to keep the fire from gaining a foothold. On the second and third floors the men worked almost wholly with buckets. Every man stuck to the post where he had been placed. There was not a whimper, though some knew their homes were in the path of the fire, and all felt there was possibly something else besides the safety of the building depending upon the issue of the contest with the great mass of fire that was soon to sweep against us. I know I had decided that, if we should be unable to withstand the heat of the flames beating against and over the building, or should be driven out by the flames taking possession of the structure, what I should try to do to preserve the lives of the brave men defending the property. I formed a plan of retreat, if the worst came, but said nothing of it to the men. If the mint building had burned it would have been warm work for us, in more than one sense, in getting outside of the fire zone, but I think we would have succeeded, for the buildings to the south of us had been burned away, so we could have gone to the streets, where we would only have had to endure the heat of the ruins until an opening was made in the fire circle surrounding us. We possibly would have had to remain inside the fire zone, like cattle in a huge corral, until the fire burned out at some point to enable us to make an exit. However, we did not have much time for speculation, or long to wait for the contest to begin. We had scarcely finished placing the men when, inside, the building was made almost dark as night by a mass of black smoke that swept in upon us just ahead of the advancing flames; then, following, came a tremendous shower of red hot cinders, big and small, which fell on our building as thick as hail in a storm, and piled up on the roof in drifts nearly two feet deep at one place against a fire wall for a distance of twenty feet. The court in the center of the building was open to the sky, and in it were much wood and timber. Here the sparks and cinders fell as thick as elsewhere, a dozen little fires were starting at various places in the court, and the men with the hose streams at each end of the court had all they could do to keep those fires down and new ones from starting. In the height of this feature of the fight I went out into the court to show a soldier who was handling one line of hose how to get the most efficiency from the stream of water. Before I could get back my clothes and hat were scorched by the falling cinders. The difficulty of keeping the fire from getting a foothold here greatly increased my fear that the mint was doomed to destruction. Finally the shower of living coals abated somewhat, making the fight in the court easier, so I passed to the upper floor, where I felt that the hardest struggle against the flames would soon take place. The buildings across the alley from the mint were on fire, and soon great masses of flames shot against the side of our building as if directed against us by a huge blow-pipe. The glass in our windows, exposed to this great heat, did not crack and break, but melted down like butter; the sandstone and granite, of which the building was constructed, began to flake off with explosive noises like the firing of artillery. The heat was now intense. It did not seem possible for the structure to withstand this terrific onslaught. The roar of the conflagration and crashing of falling buildings, together with the noises given off from the exploding stones of our building, were enough to strike terror in our hearts, if we had had time to think about it. At times the concussions from the explosions were heavy enough to make the floor quiver. Once I thought a portion of the northern wall and roof had fallen in, so loud and heavy was the crashing noise. Great tongues of flame flashed into the open windows where the glass had been melted out, and threatened to seize upon the woodwork of the interior of the tier of rooms around that side of the building. Now came the climax. Would we succeed in keeping the fire out, or should we have to retreat and leave the fire fiend to finish the destruction of the mint unhindered? Every man was alive to the situation, and with hose and buckets of water they managed to be on hand at every place when most needed—first in this room and then in that. The men in relays dashed into the rooms to play water on the flames; they met a fierce heat; though scorched was their flesh, each relay would remain in these places, which were veritable furnaces, as long as they could hold their breaths, then come out to be relieved by another crew of willing fighters. How long this particular feature of the contest went on I have little idea, but just when we thought we were getting the best of the fight another cloud of dense, black, choking smoke suddenly joined the flames and drove us back to the other end of the building, and some of the men, more sensitive to the stifling smoke, were compelled to go to the floors below. I thought the building was now doomed, beyond question, but to our surprise the smoke soon cleared up and the men, with a cheer, went dashing into the fight again. Every advantage gained by them was told by their yells of exultation. We were gaining in the fight when word came to me that the roof was now on fire and the flames were getting beyond the control of the men there, who only had buckets to fight with. The roof men wanted a hose stream, but I sent word back that the hose was needed on the third floor for a while longer and that as soon as we were out of danger at this point we would attack the roof fire from underneath in the attic. I knew the roof would burn slowly, as it was covered with copper roofing plates. The explosions of the stones in our walls grew fainter, and finally we heard no more of them. The flames ceased their efforts to find entrance to our stronghold through the windows, but the heat reflected from the mass of red hot ruins to the north of us was almost unbearable; we could not see what the situation was outside, or tell just what other or further experience was in store for us. However, we began to feel that the fight was nearly won and that, after all, we were going to save the building. We were now able to keep the interiors of the rooms which were most threatened wet down by the bucket men, so I sent the men with the hose to extinguish the roof fire, which was quickly done. In a half hour or so our defensive work was over. I now had time to take some observations, and made a trip over the building for that purpose. I found that the building had not been seriously injured, and that with careful watching and preventing the lodgment of cinders, there would be no further danger of the mint being destroyed. The fight was won. The mint was saved.

We were a happy band, pleased with the result of our efforts in successfully fighting off the fire, but we did not think so much of our victory until a day or two later when we saw the benefits to follow to the stricken community in a financial way. We opened the only available vaults in the city holding any considerable amount of coin.

It was now near 5 o'clock in the evening. The struggle with the fire demon had lasted from early morning, and all were tired, but there were other duties to be performed by them, as no relief crew was obtainable. The men were divided in watches, which gave some of them opportunity to obtain a little rest. The watch on duty was stationed at the exposed places. The hose lines were stretched, filled buckets were placed in convenient places, and steam pressure in the boiler room was ordered kept up so the fire pumps could be started at a moment's notice, if needed. When all the preparations and plans for the night had been arranged I determined to make the effort to go to Oakland and send a report to the Director of the mint at Washington, as I knew the authorities there would be pleased to know that our building had been saved. I shall never forget the feeling that came over me as I descended the steps of the mint building into Fifth Street and noted the change that had taken place there within a few short hours. When I passed down that block on Fifth Street from Market in the morning all the large business blocks, the Metropolitan Temple, and the Lincoln school were intact. The soldiers, policemen, firemen, and privileged citizens moving to and fro then gave animation to the scene, but now, turn which way you would, the view presented was one of utter ruin, desolation, and loneliness. The buildings just described were piles of smoking and blazing ruins. The street was encumbered with fallen trolley poles and tangled wires and other indestructible debris from the burned buildings. Not a human being was to be seen. It seemed as if all the people and buildings of the city but the mint and its defenders had been destroyed. It was a most depressing scene of desolation.

The heat was intense, but I picked my way through the obstacles lying in twisted and tangled masses in the street until I got out of the fire zone. I then started for the ferry at the foot of Market Street, taking something of the course on my return as that by which I came in the morning, although I had to make a wider detour to the north, as the flames had worked several blocks farther in that direction. On my way I saw that part of the fire had escaped from the firemen on Sansome Street and was racing across Kearny Street to Dupont, threatening, in its course, the destruction of Chinatown. The poor, unfortunate inmates of this section, realizing the fate in store for their homes and property, were in a state of great activity and excitement. From the speed the fire was making in their direction and the reluctance some of the Chinamen were showing in the way of leaving their homes and property, I felt that there would be a loss of life here to be added to the list of deaths caused by the disaster, but the soldiers and police came along and drove the loiterers out of the zone of danger. It was an appalling scene that I passed through on my way to the ferry. The wild march of the flames up the hill, the fleeing residents, the rushing of the firemen with their engines and trucks, and of other fire fighters to a new line of defense, the exploding charges of dynamite used to blow down buildings in the path of flame, combined in telling, in a manner stronger than words, the terrible character of the disaster the people of San Francisco were facing.

After arriving in Oakland I immediately went to the telegraph office and filed a dispatch to the Director of the mint at Washington, D. C. The telegraph office was crowded with people trying to send messages to relatives and friends. To give an idea of the extent of business suddenly thrust upon the telegraph company within the ten days following the fire, it may be said that it was unable to place all the messages filed upon the wires and hundreds were forwarded by mail. However, all government business had the right of way and was forwarded at once, so I was soon in touch with the authorities at Washington. The following is the substance of the report I sent the evening of the first day of the fire:

San Francisco visited early this morning by terrible earthquake followed by fire which has burned the greater part of business district. Mint building not damaged much by shock. Every building around the mint burned to the ground. It is the only building not destroyed for blocks. I reached building before the worst of the fire came, finding a lot of our men there, stationed them at points of vantage from roof to basement, and with our fire apparatus and without help from the fire department we successfully fought the fire away, although all the windows

Great Earthquake and Fire of 1906

on Mint Avenue and back side third story were burned out; fire coming in drove us back for a time. Adjusting rooms and refinery damaged some and heavy stone cornice on that side of building flaked off. The roof burned some little. Lieut. G. R. Armstrong, Sixth United States Infantry, with squad of men, was sent to us by commanding officer of department, who rendered efficient aid. Fire still burning in central and western parts of city, and what little remains of central business section is threatened. I could not report sooner, as I had to wait until I could return to Oakland. No dispatches could be sent from San Francisco.

There was great activity in Oakland among the people in preparing to take care of the thousands of refugees who had so suddenly and unexpectedly been thrown upon the generosity of the community. The churches and all public assembly places were thrown open to the homeless and hungry. Food, bedding, and clothing were provided as if by magic. Thousands of private homes were opened to the sufferers, and no one had occasion to complain. An intelligent organization of Oakland's leading and active citizens was effected in the shortest possible time. Lawyers, merchants, capitalists, preachers, teachers —in truth, people, men and women from all walks of life—were represented in the list of those who responded at once to aid in receiving and caring for the sufferers. Committees were sent to the depots and ferries to receive and direct the sufferers to places of refuge as fast as they arrived within the limits of Oakland. It was a grand and noble work, and was discharged with willingness and enthusiasm. It would take too much space to relate the details of the later organization and work of the citizens in caring for the refugees, the establishment of camps, and the orderly provision for the multitude of people of almost all nationalities. All I can say here is that it was well done, and a credit to the community and humanity of the people composing it.

The sudden doubling of the population of Oakland and

other conditions warranted the calling out of several companies of the National Guard to assist in policing the city, and before dusk the streets were being patrolled by soldiers. However, there was little need of them, for the circumstances of the disaster, for the time being, filled the minds of every one with only the best of thoughts and traits of character. The best that is in humanity was on parade. Strange as it may seem, it is no less a truth that life and property were never more respected or more secure than during the trying days following the disaster. All lines of class feeling were obliterated; the rich and the poor were on the one level of life. I do not remember of an instance when any individual failed to respond in the performance of duty to his fellow in distress, when and wherever called upon.

That first night of the disaster, the flames from the burning buildings in San Francisco illuminated the western part of the heavens well nigh to the zenith, and the light reflected made the streets of Oakland like twilight. Thousands of people who had been made nervous by the earthquake in the morning would not go into their homes to sleep, and either made their beds on the ground away from danger of falling walls or walked the streets. Thousands sought places of advantage from whence they could watch the progress of the conflagration on the other side of the bay. So far as weather conditions were concerned, the day and night were beautiful. This fact made it desirable and not unpleasant to be out of doors.

I retired early and had a good night's rest, which I felt was necessary, that I might be in the best trim to meet the demands my position would probably call for when I reached the mint the following day.

I reached San Francisco quite early Thursday morning. When I landed there I found the ferry building almost deserted. A policeman and two or three citizens were all the people to be seen around that usually lively place. I asked the policeman how I could best get up town. He said he did not know of any route not accompanied with danger, or without going through the fire zone. There was no way of going around the fire, as he was informed that it was then burning near the water or bay, both north and south, therefore he advised me not to try to make the trip. I asked if Market Street would not admit of a possible passage. He replied in the affirmative, and said that, if I was determined to go, that was undoubtedly the best way to get there. One of the citizens standing near, hearing the conversation, spoke up and volunteered the information that one or two parties of men had succeeded in making the trip through the burned district by following Market Street to the ferry building, although one man had been killed by falling walls and the balance of his party had been nearly suffocated by the smoke and heat from the ruins lining both sides of the street. This information was not very encouraging, but I felt that I must try to reach the mint building, as I had not heard from there since leaving the evening before, so I started out. The heat was not so great as I expected, but every now and then suffocating clouds of smoke enveloped me so closely I could hardly see or breathe. There were tons and tons of débris from all kinds of building material lying in huge masses in the street. In one or two places the fallen ruins had filled the street from curb to curb, several feet deep; these I had to clamber over, practically on "all fours." Tottering walls still stood in many places on both sides of the street. They appeared as if the slightest earthquake shock or puff of wind would send them toppling. As we had been experiencing shocks of earthquake every few hours, following the big shock, I must confess I felt I was in peril, and heartily wished I was out of that particular place. The worst of the trip was between the ferry and Montgomery Street. From Montgomery Street west to Fifth Street I had fair going, as there was but little smoke and less heat, and no débris except on the sidewalks. I was probably one of the first who passed through Market Street from the ferry, after the buildings on both sides of the street had been burned. I saw no evidence of the mishap the citizen had described to me, although I saw the dead body of a man, a victim of the fire, lying in the street near the sidewalk in front of what had been Spreckels Market. The head had nearly all been burned off, though the clothes were scarcely scorched. While about midway between Montgomery and Kearny streets on Market I noticed a small, two-story brick building still intact, which, for some strange reason, had escaped the flames that had gutted the big Crocker building to the east and the *Chronicle* building on the west and leveled the buildings between. While I stood there alone, the only person on the street, marveling as to how the building could have escaped destruction, a little jet of flame appeared above the eastern fire wall on the roof. It could have been extinguished with a bucket or two of water. I recall now that, while I saw that the building was doomed to the fate of its neighbors, it did not seem a matter of much importance. The idea probably arose from a sense of relation, wherein this building was so unconsiderable an affair, compared with the large and costly structures by which it had been surrounded, now gutted and in ruins.

I met with no other incident in completing my journey to the mint building than encountering the dead body before mentioned. I will not attempt to describe my feelings or my thoughts while making that trip up Market Street, solitary and alone, between the towering and threatening ruins of the great buildings which had lined San Francisco's main thoroughfare and amid an awful and suggestive silence. When I turned into Fifth Street quite another scene was pictured. My heart thrilled with emotion at the sight of our national colors floating from an improvised staff thrust out from the front gable peak of the mint building, the staff from which it was usually flown having been burned. The waving flag confirmed our victory over the fire demon in the contest of the day before, and proclaimed a haven of some comfort for all who could gather under its folds, and a nucleus in the restoration of the city. On the sidewalk around the building was an encampment made of all kinds of improvised shelters, occupied by several hundreds of people. In some way, they had found that the fountains in front of the building were a source of fresh water, one of the very few supplies available in the entire burned district. As the sidewalks and the two lawn spaces in front of the building offered a camping place, as many as could be accommodated located there. Having an abundant supply of fresh water in our wells, I had a couple of pipe lines run to convenient places near the sidewalk, and for two or three days there were lines of people awaiting their turns at the faucets. Among the campers I found some acquaintances and some guests from the St. Francis Hotel. The mint people did all within their power to make the refugees comfortable. One or two sick people were given shelter in the building for the night.

The mint now being out of danger, I sent the following message to the Director of the mint:

SAN FRANCISCO, April 19, 1906.
(Forwarded from Oakland.)

As feared, the balance of the business part of the city was destroyed last night. The fire is now raging in the western residence section. Whole street is now being dynamited across the path of the fire. The mint building safe, one side scaled by heat, but interior is intact. It is the only building in path of fire south of Market not destroyed, except new postoffice partially burned. Apprehend no further trouble from fire.

The squad of soldiers stood watch with our men, but managed in some way to get hold of liquor during the night, and one or two of them became intoxicated and, consequently, troublesome. One of them threatened to shoot the doorkeeper who had refused to allow him to go out of the building, acting under the directions of the army officer in charge of the soldiers. I was sent for, as it appeared there was going to be serious trouble. When I arrived on the scene the troublesome soldier was loading his rifle. He threatened to close my earthly career if I took another step nearer or interfered with his purposes. It was an ugly situation, but I succeeded in quieting the fellow and induced him to unload his gun. I then found the sergeant in charge of the squad and requested him to take the men away, as we were now able to take care of the building without outside help. This was about the only incident worthy of mention occurring on the second day in the mint. A regular watch of two hours on and four off, on duty inside and outside of the building, was established. The officers of the mint passed a good part of the day on the roof, watching the progress of the fire.

The next morning I received several telegrams, among which were two from the Secretary of the Treasury—one asking for a statement as to the loss of life and extent of damage and the condition of banks in neighboring towns, and the other thanking us for saving the mint building, and complimenting our actions. He also requested me to recommend some action that would enable the department to relieve the situation. In response, I replied by wire that the stories of loss of life had been grossly exaggerated, that I had been in position to hear from all parts of the city, and I did not think the list of the dead would reach more than 400; that the fire did not travel fast and the authorities took trouble to keep ahead of the flames, notifying people of the danger, and caring for the helpless. "Every bank in San Francisco buried in ruins. All banks in Oakland, Berkeley, and Alameda able to resume business. To meet the conditions the suburban banks ought to have free and prompt telegraphic transfer of funds. In view of the ruined condition of sub-treasury, I advise making transfers direct through the mint." I also reported that the fire was practically under control and that it was estimated that about half of the residence section would be saved from the flames.

The suggestion to make free transfer of funds by telegraph was promptly adopted, and the Secretary wisely extended the privilege to individuals in private life. This action proved far-reaching in re-establishing a financial system and restoring confidence in the banking institutions of the city, that had been temporarily put out of business, to say nothing of the relief afforded people in private life. The procedure in the transfer of money was made very simple. A person or firm in the East desiring to have a given sum of money delivered to a person, firm, or corporation in San Francisco, or any part of the state, would deposit the amount at any of the sub-treasuries of the United States, giving the name and address of the person to whom it was to be delivered. These particulars would be telegraphed to me, and I would send notices to the beneficiaries to call at the mint and receive the money. Some idea as to the extent people used the privilege accorded by the government can be formed by the statement that over $40,000,000 was transferred in less than a fortnight. The transfers ranged in sums from $50 to over $1,000,000 each. On the first day of the transfers I attended to the business without assistance; however, the next day, I had to have the help of a couple of clerks, and in two or three days after the transfers had so increased in number that the work required the help of all the clerks in the mint force. Not a dollar was lost. Only one payment, a $300 transfer, was delivered to the wrong person. The person who received it bore the same name and initials as the party for whom it was intended. The error was discovered soon

Sunday after the Fire

THE United States Mint Building as it appeared immediately after the fire, showing the temporary shelters of the refugees located around the structure. The national flag is seen displayed on a temporary staff from the gable peak. The halyards and top of the regular staff were burned when the fire swept over the building on the first day of the disaster.

after the payment was made, and the money was returned at once. Not more than two or three transfers were returned to the senders as "not called for."

On the morning of the fourth day, or on April 21, I was able to report to the Washington authorities that all fire had been extinguished or had burned out for the lack of buildings to burn. Referring to the establishment of a bureau of information, requested by the Secretary of the Treasury at the suggestion of people anxious to learn of the condition of relatives and friends in the ill-fated city, I reported that I found that the relief committees, both in San Francisco and Oakland, were trying to accomplish the purpose with the aid of the Associated Press, though the manager of the Western Union Telegraph Company informed me that he thought the plan impracticable at that time, as it would be impossible to get the desired information over the wires, which were then more than forty-eight hours behind in forwarding the ordinary messages filed. I also suggested "that reassuring telegrams be spread through the country, explaining that stories of loss of lives and condition of people had been grossly exaggerated." I further stated that the list of dead and injured "was exceedingly small, considering character and extent of the disaster. No further danger, unless the conflagration should break out anew. Officials declare they have affairs completely in hand. Relief supplies are coming in rapidly, and everybody is being taken care of. Water mains being repaired."

Up to this time, business of all kinds had been suspended in Oakland and other towns of the bay section, but now the care of the homeless and helpless had been systematized, and circumstances required that the banks and business houses be opened again to supply the needs of the general community of the state. Business throughout the entire state had been paralyzed. All confidence in the stability of the banks was for the time suspended.

Depositors could not withdraw any part of their funds, nor could they induce any one to cash their checks. Realizing that one of the greatest aids in relief of the condition was to re-establish the San Francisco sub-treasury, I therefore got hold of Assistant Treasurer Jacobs, gave him quarters in the mint building, and advanced him all the money he needed, thus starting him in business without waiting for authority from Washington, being satisfied that the emergency warranted my action and that the Secretary of the Treasury would approve the act, which he did, subsequently. For the same reason I also gave the commandant at Mare Island navy yard $50,000 with which to pay the workmen there. The Selby Smelting and Lead Company was probably the distributor of the greatest amount of actual cash of any business agency on the Coast. I sent word to the manager to establish an office in the mint building and resume the purchases of bullion, and we would take it off the company's hands at once. This arrangement was the means of sending out into various parts of the state an average of $225,000 daily.

One of the most difficult problems confronting the business interests of this city was the re-establishment of the banking business that would give some kind of a financial system at once. People had begun to feel the need of the money buried in the vaults of the banks. There was no telling how long before these vaults could be opened. The banks, to meet the wants, had funds transferred from points in the East to their credit at the mint, but there was no place where they could keep this money and open up for business. A committee of the bankers' association came to me to arrange to check against their credits in favor of their clients, but that was impossible, for we had no men trained in the banking business to do the work, nor suitable books. After some discussion of the subject, I proposed that the association should organize an emergency, or central, bank representing all the banks of the city, using the funds in the mint to their credit as the capital for the emergency bank, the banking institutions forming this central bank to establish offices in various parts of the city, where they could issue checks on the central bank in favor of their clients, the central bank to be officered by men of their own selection. I told the committee that, if such plans met with their approval, I would supply ample quarters in the mint suitable for the transaction of the business. The plan was adopted and worked out splendidly, meeting all requirements and remaining in operation for several weeks, until the various banks were able to open up in their individual capacity. This accommodation to the bankers and to the public was one of the benefits arising from the saving of the mint building from destruction, making available the three hundred and odd millions of dollars in the vaults there. We received many expressions of appreciation of the favors granted by the Treasury Department and delight that the mint had been preserved to render such great accommodation to the people of the state in the time of its greatest necessity.

President Roosevelt increased my duties and responsibilities by requesting me to act as custodian of relief funds, then being collected in the various parts of the country and forwarded to San Francisco. To handle this money necessitated the detail of a couple of clerks and several assistants. The money came to us in all shapes, from nickels to big bills. One donation of $5000 from a street railroad company was all in nickels. In one day alone we received fifty-one packages of money from all parts of the United States which took nearly two days to count. However, I was relieved of this duty soon after the general relief committee was organized.

I had to arrange to house and feed a lot of our men whose places of abode had been destroyed; besides, many of the guards had to remain at the building, as it was difficult to go and come any distance. I obtained a supply of bedding and provisions from stores in Oakland. Some of our workmen understood cooking, so we soon had an efficient restaurant established in the building. One day we fed 124 people at the noon meal. The restaurant was continued until places outside were established, relieving us of the necessity of feeding the employees.

By Saturday night our electricians had improvised an electric light plant, by changing one of our large motors into a generator, which enabled us to supply a current sufficient to light up the interior of the building and the streets around the building. This gave some appearance of cheerfulness at night in the field of desolation and ruin around us, and was especially agreeable to the many people encamped in our neighborhood. On Sunday I reported to the authorities at Washington as follows:

We will open for business Monday, receiving deposits and paying out transfer funds. All men of mint force accounted for but four. Will have to furnish subsistence for employees for some little time, getting principal supplies from army headquarters, only buying such things as can not be obtained there. Much activity in city preparatory to resumption of business. Last of fire extinguished during night; relief supplies coming in abundance. People generally in comfortable condition. Relief committee patrolling streets hunting for distressed.

On April 23, or the following day, I was able to report that every man of the mint force had been accounted for, and that the United States Signal Corps had run a wire into the mint building and established an office there, putting us in direct connection with the rest of the world.

As soon as the minds of the people reverted to the subject of renewal of business and the reopening of the obstructed streets to permit the operation of the street railroad lines, the city authorities placed a crew of men in the burned district, blowing down standing ruins of brick buildings with dynamite, and other crews of men were set to work clearing the streets of debris. For the latter work it was difficult to obtain all the laborers needed, therefore citizens, regardless of station or occupation, were impressed, through aid of soldiers, and were made to donate about a half hour's labor before being released. Nearly everybody caught and put to work made light of the affair, but now and then some of the impressed created a scene. A young lawyer from one of our neighboring states, who had come to San Francisco to gratify his curiosity by viewing the ruins of the city, was one of the captured who was not excused from performing the task allotted to him. He made violent protest, and his feelings were so outraged that he did not miss an opportunity to denounce all officials, state and city, for several years thereafter.

The work of dynamiting was conducted in a most unskilful manner, doing considerable damage to the structures that had wholly or partially escaped destruction in the conflagration. It was necessary that the tottering walls remaining from the ruins of many of the large buildings along the principal thoroughfares should be leveled before the people could with safety use the streets, or the street cars be allowed to run. Nearly all the class "A" buildings were intact, so far as the walls and floors were concerned, and offered no menace. It was the buildings constructed before the introduction of steel frames that supplied the menacing piles of brick, and it was this kind of structures that predominated in the business section of the city.

The crew of dynamiters apparently had little knowledge of the use of explosives, and less experience. They seemed to work on the principle that, if a small amount of powder was good, a large amount would be better. About the first work they attempted was the demolishing of the standing walls of what had been the Odd Fellows' Building at the corner of Seventh and Market streets.

They set off so much dynamite there that they not only threw down the walls intended to be leveled, but the force of the explosion blew in all the windows of the post-office building, a block away from the scene of the explosion, besides which many doors were torn from their hinges and much of the marble work of the structure was displaced and broken. I was told by Mr. J. W. Roberts, assistant to the United States supervising architect, that one blast of dynamite did more damage than was occasioned by the fire and earthquake together, and that the cost of repairs to the building was made $100,000 greater by reason of the careless work. The mint building was damaged also on this occasion, and further injury was inflicted by subsequent blasting done nearer to our building, not a pane of glass being left whole. I recovered a piece of iron, about a quarter of a pound in weight, that was thrown by a blast set off nearly a quarter of a mile away and which landed in our court, as well as pieces of iron bolts and fragments of bricks that landed on or in the building from other blasts. I made a vigorous protest against this manner of blasting, and at the same time offered to supply men experienced in the use of explosives, guaranteeing that the work would be executed thoroughly and quickly, without danger to the people or property, but no attention was paid to my protest or offer. I then sent a communication to Mayor Schmitz containing a protest in about the same terms. He promptly replied, saying: "I shall take great pleasure in having your request complied with. I will have the man in charge of the dynamiting of the unsafe walls call upon you tomorrow morning and will instruct him to arrange matters satisfactory to you."

The man called the "next morning," not to "arrange matters," but apparently to show his independence and his defiance of all authority, for all that he had to say was to look out for ourselves, as he was going to throw down the walls of the big Emporium building that forenoon. Being certain that the walls of that building were in no danger of falling and consequently could not menace traffic, and that to dynamite them was not only useless and would result in injury to government property, but was an outrage on the owners of the Emporium building, I repeated my protest to General Funston, then in charge of the troops and representing the government here. He promptly sent a colonel, whose name I do not now recall, with a couple of troopers to confer with me and empowered to act. It was then late in the forenoon. The dynamiters had been working up Market Street toward the Emporium, with apparent determination to carry out their purpose of demolishing that structure, or what was left of it. The concussions from the blasting were so heavy that injury to our building in some form followed every explosion. The falling material placed the lives of those in and about the mint in great danger, and we were compelled to suspend the work of repairs. When I explained the situation to the colonel he was inclined to take issue with me, intimating that we were unnecessarily alarmed. While he was trying to assure me there was no danger to be apprehended and that work was in good hands, etc., a tremendous blast under the ruins of the old Phelan Block was set off. Although this explosion was located nearly a quarter of a mile away, a shower of missiles fell in our vicinity; the vibrations were most severe; the crashing of falling glass in the mint building was terrific. The colonel involuntarily ducked his head as if he were dodging the explosion of a 14-inch shell. It was unnecessary for me to make reply to his arguments. I simply looked at him, my countenance undoubtedly wearing a significant expression of "didn't I tell you so?" The colonel, upon regaining his composure, in a very gentlemanly way acknowledged his error and said he would stop the outrageous work at once. He prevented the destruction of the Emporium walls and all further heavy blasting in the vicinity of the mint. It may be of interest to note that the imposing front of the present big Emporium building is the same front that passed through the earthquake and fire, which was doomed to be leveled by the inexperienced crew of dynamiters. We were now able to resume repairs on our building and transact business. The mint was the center of all financial affairs. Its halls and corridors were filled during business hours with people called there by business requirements. They were making use of the privileges and benefits arising from the preservation of the mint building and the great stock of money in its vaults. I do not know what would have happened had the mint suffered the fate of the other financial institutions. The banks were timid enough as it was with the mint funds available, and the condition was made worse by some disturbance of confidence in the banks. Within a week after the fire the streets of San Francisco presented a remarkable scene of life and activity; teams of every description, crowds of people on foot coming and going in all directions, gangs of men at work clearing away the debris from the streets, some at work erecting temporary structures in which to resume business, others engaged in making repairs on gas and water pipes, restoring telegraph and power lines, and laying railroad tracks through the burned district to facilitate the removal of debris. Everybody seemed busy, and all wore expressions of determination, as well as confidence in the future greatness of San Francisco.

In sweeping over the business section the fire performed some strange antics. A small two-story brick building on the northwest corner of Second and Mission streets was scarcely scorched; a canvas awning used for a shelter for a cigar stand there was only partially destroyed; the window panes were left intact, and the merchandise inside the structure was uninjured. I was told that the first information the owner of the property had of the remarkable incident was when a friend congratulated him on his good fortune, about a week after the fire. He had supposed the place went the way of everything else in that part of the city, and had not attempted to visit it. On the Second Street side, as well as on the Mission Street side of the little building, were located extra tall buildings, both of which were gutted by the fire, but in some way they served to protect their little neighbor from the conflagration.

A tall office building on Montgomery Street had its lower and upper stories burned out, while the three or four floors between wholly escaped all damage from the flames; the lucky occupants of the offices on these floors found their possessions, books, and papers undamaged. An entire block of buildings bounded by Montgomery, Sansome, Jackson, and Merchant streets was passed by the flames, while all else in the neighborhood except the United States Appraiser's building in the east block adjoining was laid low by the devouring elements. This was the business center of the city in early days, and the large old-fashioned brick building in the district described was the largest and most important structure in the city for some years and was known as the Montgomery Block, and some of the adjoining structures were among the very oldest buildings in San Francisco. After the fire, for a few months, the old Montgomery Block was once more a place of importance and a center of business activity, such as it had not known for a score or more of years.

For several weeks after the disaster the streets of that part of the city escaping the fire presented novel scenes arising from the fact that all housekeepers were obliged to cook their meals in the street. The city authorities would not allow lights or fire of any kind to be used in any of the houses until they were inspected. When all leaking gaspipes and damaged chimneys had been found and repaired, certificates were issued by the inspector permitting the use of lights and fires in the houses. The cooking or kitchen devices that fronted nearly every residence on the street were greatly varied in form. Some had quite elaborate kitchens, with ingenious arrangements of bricks for service as range or stoves, while others were satisfied with the most primitive outfits. The rule was strictly enforced; the guards and police were given instructions to even shoot if necessary to secure compliance with the ordinance. The utmost vigilance was used to prevent the breaking out of fires in this part of the city until the water mains were repaired and the fire department re-established. The people were extremely nervous, as well they might be, for if another fire had started, with no water, and a disorganized fire department, the remainder of the city would undoubtedly have been swept by flames.

There was considerable difference in the estimates made as to the number of fatalities resulting from the earthquake and the fire following. At the request of Secretary Shaw of the Treasury Department, I looked into this feature of the disaster with care and sent him reports from time to time of my findings and conclusions. At first, or a few days after the fire had been extinguished, my figures on the total of those killed outright and those who died from the result of injuries received only reached a number of about four hundred, but after the ruins cooled off, in the work of clearing away the debris in the burned district, the remains of other unfortunates were found, adding somewhat more than a hundred to the list of fatalities. In my final report to the Secretary, I fixed the number of killed at approximately five hundred people. The record as kept by the city authorities exceeded my figures, as I remember, by fifteen or twenty. Undoubtedly these figures were near the truth, and they would fix the ratio of deaths by the disaster at but a trifle over one person to each thousand of population. The greatest number of deaths at any one place occurred on Valencia Street, where a three-story frame hotel building was thrown down by the earthquake. The first and second stories appeared to have telescoped and were then crushed flat by the weight of the third story, which practically retained its shape as it sank down on the wreck below. The dead and injured were removed some time before the fire swept that section. The number killed was reported at twenty-seven. The hotel had been erected on a piece of filled ground, where the effect of the earthquake was most severely felt. The piece of filled ground was less than a block wide and extended from the hills to the bay. After the earthquake the outlines of the filled section could be traced for the entire distance by the wrecked buildings located on it.

It was very remarkable how quickly on that first morning an efficient organization was effected for the care and treatment of the hundreds of injured people. Temporary hospitals, with physicians, surgeons, nurses, and help, were provided like magic in various parts of the city. One or two of these hospitals were compelled to remove their patients once or twice to avoid the course of the flames. I do not recall ever having seen an official statement of the number of injured treated; but from conversation with some of those who officiated in the hospitals I formed the opinion that the total would not exceed fifteen hundred persons.

THE RELIEF WORK

There was no delay in giving relief to the homeless sufferers. The people in San Francisco who escaped from the earthquake and fire seemed to know at once their duty to the unfortunates, and how to perform it without suggestions. That inborn power of leadership with which nature endows a man here and there, only to be made manifest and exercised in crises and great emergencies, gave an immediate supply of leaders and directors at several points in the city, without the formality of selection or other means. The badge of natural leadership was quickly recognized by the common workers. There were places of refuge made at once for the sick and the injured, and food provided for the hungry. In the course of a few days the temporary relief measures gave way to control by most complete organizations on both sides of the bay, which were maintained for several months, or until all need of their work was ended.

It will never be known how much was the money or what the value of the goods and provisions contributed for the relief of the sufferers, as so much relief work was given directly to the needy, and through agencies and organizations other than the ones under the direction and control of the municipal authorities. Not a few firms and individuals chose to expend what they had to contribute in the earliest stages of the crisis by direct distribution to the needy or in other ways to relieve the situation. Many social, fraternal, and similar organizations, which sought to aid in relief work, preferred to have their contributions go directly to suffering or unfortunate members of their societies.

Many thousands of dollars were raised in Oakland and other cities near San Francisco, and expended by relief associations in those communities, for the care of refugees from San Francisco. These amounts were not and could not be accounted for in the statements of disbursements by the San Francisco relief committee. In Oakland alone, the local relief organizations expended $100,000 of its own collections in addition to $10,000 given to it by the San Francisco organization. The Standard Oil Company established and maintained a camp for the care of the helpless and homeless near Richmond at its own cost, the expenditures not being accounted for nor made a part

Great Earthquake and Fire of 1906

of the total expended by the general relief committee of San Francisco.

In the month that I acted as treasurer and custodian of the general relief funds, from April 27, I received from contributors in San Francisco, the state, United States, and foreign countries, the sum of $2,409,656.35. A large part of this sum was disbursed on orders from the proper officials of the general relief committee. When several of the large banking firms were able to resume business on June 1, I insisted upon being relieved of the responsibility of handling these funds, and turned over the balance to the banks designated for the purpose.

The actual cash remitted direct to San Francisco and accounted for by the Relief Association was $8,921,452.86, and additional funds were acquired from the sale of surplus and perishable relief supplies, interest, etc., to the extent of $751,605.08, making a grand total of $9,673,057.94.

In addition to what has been enumerated, nearly $50,000 was expended by the Red Cross Society in Washington, from San Francisco relief subscriptions, and the government appropriation of $2,500,000 was disbursed entirely by and under direction of the War Department, principally for bedding, tents, medical supplies, maintenance of relief camps, food, clothing, etc. Neither was the value of the two thousand carloads of food supplies, clothing, etc., ever computed in dollars and cents. In all probability the total amount disbursed in relief work, counted in money, if ever it could be determined, would reach a sum somewhere between fourteen and fifteen millions of dollars.

The larger part of this great sum was contributed within the United States. Contributions from other countries would have been generous but for the proclamation of President Roosevelt practically declining aid from outside countries. Nevertheless, England, France, Germany, Japan, and Mexico were represented in the list of contributors, Japan being the largest, sending nearly a quarter million of dollars. The emperor of that country gave about $100,000 of the amount himself. One of the most noteworthy features of this record of generosity and expression of world-wide human sympathy was the contribution in the stricken city itself of the sum of $413,090 by the citizens and business men there, nearly all of whom had themselves been injured in property losses. Undoubtedly there were other contributions of money and supplies from this source which were not reported or handed in to the general committee, but were made directly by the donors, and which would swell the total of San Francisco's donations to its sufferers to more than a half million of dollars.

The particulars of how the relief funds were expended would fill a volume of large size. All the people whose homes were destroyed were not helpless. Many of them were people of means, and there were many who soon found refuge with relations or friends in the unburned district of the city and elsewhere. So, after the first few days of the disaster, the number of refugees depending upon the relief committee was reduced to the helpless as well as the homeless, of which there were estimated to be some 30,000, but by the latter part of September, following the fire, the number of refugees being cared for by the committee was about 18,000. Some fifteen or twenty camps were established in various parts of the city. When it was found that the relief committee would of necessity have to care for several thousand helpless people for several months to come, the camps were made in the most comfortable shape, tents were floored, the grounds were put in the most complete sanitary condition and scrupulous cleanliness was enforced by army officers. Hot and cold water and bathhouses were provided in all the camps. Before the winter was over, wooden shacks and small cottages largely replaced the tents.

It was frequently remarked that many of the inmates of those camps enjoyed more comforts than they had been accustomed to; but no one begrudged them that. It was a satisfaction to know that all efforts to make the unfortunates comfortable in healthy and pleasant surroundings were so successful.

In addition to the camps, some ten or twelve kitchens and eating places were established in July in various parts of the city by the relief committee. These places furnished meals at low prices to those able to pay. Those who were unable to pay presented meal tickets supplied under authority of the relief committee. During the first month the kitchens furnished 20,867 meals, but by the end of September, or the third month, many privately owned restaurants had been established and the need of the public kitchen was no longer felt, so these latter institutions were discontinued.

The relief committee was composed of some of the most successful and prominent business men and capitalists in San Francisco, and they brought to the organization the very best talent for the kind of work in hand. They knew what was needed and how to accomplish it. After housing the homeless, they began the more serious and difficult work of replacing these people in their former positions in the industrial world. Hundreds of sewing-machines were given outright to women who needed them to earn a livelihood, and to other women who had large families to care for. Many thousands of dollars were expended for mechanics' tools given to men to enable them to find employment at their various trades.

Nearly one million of dollars was expended in building new dwellings to aid those whose homes had been burned. This was one of the very creditable and successful features of the relief work. By aid received the committee effected the construction of over eight thousand dwellings in the city. The requirements of this work prolonged the labors of the committee nearly two years after the camp system was discontinued. The remnant of the refugees by August, 1908, was only about seven hundred, all aged and infirm. The committee constructed a permanent home for these unfortunates and gave it to the city, and the municipal authorities then assumed the care of the building and inmates.

The final report of the relief committee was filed January 4, 1911.

The relief work described was repeated in Oakland and other cities around the bay along the same lines, but not on so large a scale.

LOSSES AND RECONSTRUCTION

The territory swept by the conflagration measured four miles in length in a northerly and southerly course by three miles in width east and west. Every bank, every theater, every hotel of importance, all newspaper offices, telegraph offices, libraries, municipal buildings, and nearly all of the business houses in San Francisco were destroyed by the conflagration. The value of the property thus wiped out of existence was placed near five hundred millions of dollars. About one-half of the loss was recovered through insurance. San Francisco was struck a staggering blow, but, fortunately, the people of San Francisco were in the best condition to meet it. For some time past the city had been enjoying a wonderful degree of prosperity. The business section was handling the greatest volume of trade it had ever known. Mechanics and laborers were all employed, receiving the best of wages. Building was going on at a greater rate than ever known before. Real estate values were advancing most rapidly, making old-timers wag their heads with astonishment. In every direction the city was expanding and on every

UPPER—The north side of the United States Mint Building, showing how the fire scarred the walls.
LOWER—A scene of desolation taken a few days after the fire from the roof of the United States Mint, looking northwesterly.

hand there was evidence of thrift and prosperity. The banks were in the best of condition, proof of which lies in the fact that when the disaster came they had over twenty millions of surplus coin on deposit in banks of the Eastern cities.

The majority of the people who saw their businesses swept away by the fire were financially able to resume the struggle with the world, and naturally the question of where to begin came to them. Where?

Should it be in New York, where business is conducted on the lines of keenest competition, and where every phase of living is in such direct contrast to the freedom enjoyed by Californians? Or in Chicago, Philadelphia, Boston, Baltimore, or similar cities, where the conditions of home life might be better than in the city of the Empire State, but business conditions for a stranger and newcomer would be more complex? Everywhere it would be a beginning among strangers—a crowding in where the fight of the "survival of the fittest" was always on. At best, the establishing of a business elsewhere would be experimental.

It only required a moment's consideration of the opportunities at home to settle the question. San Francisco was the place for them, where they were known and where there were still over three hundred thousand people to be fed, clothed, and housed. Here there was an adjacent country big enough for an empire, and as rich in possibilities as any land on God's footstool, for which San Francisco was the bank and clearing house, the shipping point for the products, and the supply house for the needs. San Francisco was the place for them, for had not the commercial hand of the Orient and the islands been reaching out to this port, taking more and more of the things we grow and make, and returning to us things that the people of the Occident crave and need? San Francisco then was the place to renew business, where the conditions not only invited but demanded it, with the promise of great profit.

The decision was instantly made, and before the smoke of the conflagration had entirely blown away, or the heat passed out of the fallen debris, the noise and activities attending the cleaning and rebuilding amid the ruins were heard and seen on every hand. The banks quickly quartered themselves in makeshift structures built around their undamaged vaults, and sent for their millions in New York and elsewhere, to be properly prepared for the unusual drafts anticipated on their surplus. But, to the great surprise of all, the banks upon opening received more money on deposit than they paid out! That the trade of the great country tributary to San Francisco and the adjoining states might not suffer, and that the people of our city might be furnished with the necessities of life and supplies for rehabilitating the city, it was apparent that the first thing to be done was to order goods and prepare temporary structures in which to house them and the people engaged in business. All over the burned district these structures began to make their appearance. They were not all pretty and not all homely, but sufficient and suitable for the purposes intended. Trainloads of goods began to arrive and the new stores and warehouses were filled up as fast as completed. Within a marvelously short time, the streets of the city, the water front, and the depots of the Southern Pacific and the Santa Fé companies showed the life of trade and commerce. The erection of buildings continued, the volume of trade increased, and the incoming freight crowded upon the merchants faster than they could take it away. The main business streets, from early morn to night, presented daily one continual procession of teams laden with goods, coming and going. A great many retailers and professional men located in that part of the city between Van Ness Avenue and Fillmore Street, which escaped the fire, the former street becoming the location for the larger and more important retail business houses. For some time afterwards it was a much discussed question whether or not these firms would remain there permanently, and thus bring around a radical change of the business center of the city. Van Ness Avenue, being a wide and beautiful street, presented a lively and attractive appearance while trade was located there, but as soon as new permanent buildings were erected down town in the old retail section, and office buildings were restored, the stores and professional men returned to the neighborhood where they had transacted business in the years before the fire, and the district that had given them temporary accommodation was largely restored to use for private residences. Van Ness Avenue became the automobile mart of the city. Fillmore Street, however, was a business street before the fire, and it did not lose much by the return of business firms to their old locations down town. Immediately after the conflagration, when people began to discuss the subject of replacing the buildings destroyed by the fire, there was expressed much difference of opinion as to the time it would take. Many thought that such a gigantic undertaking could not be accomplished inside of twenty years, and I think ten years was most commonly fixed upon as the length of time required. When asked for my judgment, I said that after five years people would have to hunt around the business section of San Francisco to find any remaining evidence of the great disaster. Considering the matter eight years after the terrible event, it must be admitted that I was nearly correct as to the time in which the business section would be restored, yet it must be acknowledged that the entire burned district had not been rebuilt. The old residential section north of Market is being rehabilitated with apartment houses, giving place to the possibilities of a much denser population than existed in the same boundaries before the fire. In the district bounded by Market, Mason, California, and Larkin streets there is probably more than a quarter of the area still uncovered, but the fine, large apartment houses and hotels that have taken the sites of former residences and flats are housing in the same area possibly ten times as many people as were living there before the fire. There are still many vacant lots in the old cheap tenement district south of Mission Street which are slowly coming into occupation for warehouses, factories, and cheap boarding and lodging houses. San Francisco lost heavily in population by the conflagration. I should judge by an estimate from the number of votes cast before and after at elections, and the statistics furnished by the school census, that fully one-third of the people living in San Francisco, through fear of recurrence of earthquakes, loss of homes, property and like reasons, left the city with the idea of permanently abandoning the place. Not a few of these people in the course of time undoubtedly changed their minds and returned to the city. These, with the newcomers, gave a fairly rapid growth to the population, but the number of the population before the fire was hardly restored until five years after the disaster.

STRANGE EFFECTS

There were numerous instances of remarkable and queer mental disturbances in individuals caused by their experience in those four days of fire, the earthquake on April 18, and the seven lesser shocks that followed on that and subsequent days. People who were apparently sane and rational on all other matters would relate scenes of accident, robbery, and violence, wholesale slaughter of people by falling buildings, fire, and by shooting by the soldiers, etc. Stories of mutilation of the dead by ghoulish robbers, for earrings and finger rings were most common and for a time were generally accepted as being true, but I never learned of a single authenticated instance of such a crime. In one case a story came to my ears with much detail of facts of how a man was caught in the act of cutting off the fingers of a victim of the fire to obtain some valuable rings, and when his clothes were searched a pocketful of human fingers was found; then and there his captors promptly punished the criminal with death by hanging. The circumstances were alleged to have taken place at a point quite near to the mint. I was therefore enabled to make an investigation and I found that there was not the slightest foundation for the story. An afternoon newspaper gave credit to an absurd story that the mint had been assailed by a band of robbers in broad daylight, but that the guards or watchmen employed by the government had succeeded in defeating the attempt at robbery, and in accomplishing this they killed at least eleven of the robbers, whose dead bodies were left where they fell. Of course the facts were related with much more detail than attempted here. It was not so very strange that a newspaper should publish an unwarranted yarn like this, and I am only referring to it here as an instance in support of the opening words of this paragraph. This will be understood by the statement that on the evening of the publication my son Harry was refuting the story to a coterie of acquaintances, when a stranger standing near, overhearing his denial, interrupted him, saying that he was wrong and that the story *was* true, for he saw the affray himself, witnessing the shooting and seeing some of the men fall. The reported attack was as baseless as it was untrue. There was no attack; there was no row or even a dispute on the mint steps or about the building. One man told me, with considerable emotion (I think it was on the fourth day after the earthquake), that he had occasion to go over into the northern part of the burned district, and in order to reach a particular place he was compelled to pass through a block where the dead bodies of earthquake victims still lay so thick that he had difficulty in getting along without stepping on some of them. As I was gathering facts on which to base a report of the fatalities, at the request of the Secretary, I made an investigation of this statement and found it to be like the others described—without foundation. On returning home from the mint Thursday night about dusk, I stood on the rear deck of the ferry boat, discussing with a well-known newspaper correspondent the progress of the fire and the possibilities of getting it under control. Reaching the station at Seventh and Broadway, we walked up the street, when he suddenly remarked, "That was a terrible sight, wasn't it?" I asked him to what he referred. "Why, the burning of the ferry building as we left it, with the people trapped in there," said he. I replied that it could hardly be so, as there was no fire within a mile of the building at that time. He looked at me with astonishment, and said that he could not understand why I did not see it, for he had watched the flames lapping up the great structure, from his position on the boat all the way across the bay, and that we had scarcely left the slip when the fire burst out from many places in the building, and it was so sudden that undoubtedly hundreds of people in the building must have been caught and burned to death. I saw by his manner and expression that he was so certain of the truth of what he had stated that it would be unprofitable to discuss the matter further with him. More than likely, reporters affected in the same strange way were the parties responsible for the many wild, baseless, and lurid reports of the doings of the earthquake and fire, published not only in our state but throughout all parts of the world reached by telegraphic service. At the time of the disaster there was no motive for resorting to "fake" statements, for there were more facts and details of truth, sensational in character, than place or space could be found for in any newspaper. Only a disordered brain could account for the publication of hourly bulletins in a nearby city, describing with horrible detail the gradual submergence in the waters of the bay of Oakland, Berkeley, and Alameda, accompanied by a terrible loss of life. Such, however, is a sample of hundreds of baseless reports of features of the great disaster that found publication in all parts of the United States. I can not believe they were wilfully made by the reporters with knowledge that they were untrue.

LOSSES AND INSURANCE

The exact value of the property destroyed in the disaster will never be known. The fire swept over the city too quickly to give an opportunity to survey the havoc wrought by the earthquake alone. While the damage from this source was considerable, it probably was not a hundredth part of the total losses made by the fire that followed. In a recent discussion of the fire loss with George W. Dornin, one of the best informed insurance men on the Pacific Coast, he gave some figures confirming the estimate made by business men soon after the disaster, which was that the total property loss, not including contingent losses, such as disruption of business, was somewhere between $400,000,000 and $500,000,000. The exact amount of insurance on the property was not known. It could only be approximated, and this was estimated at from $200,000,000 to $225,000,000. As near as could be determined, $164,916,659 was paid to the insured on their losses, which sum included the amount recovered in after years from companies which litigated the losses. Mr. Dornin estimated that the defaulted insurance amounted to about $8,000,000.

Fire patrol statistics for a series of years show that the uninsured loss equals the insured loss, so that if the estimate of the amount of insurance in force, $200,000,000, is correct, it would indicate the total loss in the great conflagration was double the amount, or $400,000,000. Of the insurance paid, California companies paid over $11,000,000, other American companies nearly $83,000,000, and foreign companies nearly $71,000,000.

CORRESPONDENCE

I conclude my story of the earthquake and fire by appending copies of a few of the letters I received and replies made, which may give some additional interest to the history of the great disaster, as well as make clearer some of the situations I attempted to describe. There is also included copy of a letter sent by an employee of the mint, Joe Hammill, to his brother, which gives a vivid description of how the United States mint building was saved. It follows:

SAN FRANCISCO, May 11, 1906.

DEAR BROTHER—You have heard many conflicting accounts of how the United States mint was saved, and I want you to know the exact facts as they were, as I saw them on April 18.

When the earthquake at 5:15 A. M. rocked the city, hundreds of buildings south of Market Street were either thrown down or badly shattered. The mint, however, escaped serious damage, though its great chimneys are both badly cracked and seem to lean toward the center of the building, where a great court is located. Small chimneys were thrown in every direction and furniture overturned. Fire broke out shortly after the earthquake and by 9 o'clock the entire district south of Mission was a mass of fire, which leaped from block to block as though running through dry grass. It swept Mission Street clean, scorching the south side of the mint but doing no great damage, for the iron shutters on the windows shielded the inner woodwork of the offices and melting room.

Superintendent Frank A. Leach arrived at the mint from Oakland early in the morning, and immediately took charge of operations. Through his coolness and ability the men under him worked to the best advantage. He took his turn at the hose with the others, and did not ask his men to go where he would not go himself. It is remarkable how he has stood the strain of the fire and press of business since.

About fifty of the mint employees succeeded in reaching the building before the soldiers barred the way to all comers. Then a detachment of artillerymen, commanded by Lieutenant G. W. Armstrong of the Sixth Infantry, entered the building to serve more as a guard than as a band of firefighters. Later, Lieutenant Armstrong and a few of his men did take an active part. . . .

Within the yard of the mint is an artesian well which proved the only water available. The pump connections were badly broken by the earthquake, yet the engineer, Jack Brady, did a lightning job in repairing the pumping plant, making connections in short order that ordinarily would require a long time. He finished his splendid work just in time to supply the fire fighters with two streams of water.

Meanwhile the fire swept up Fifth Street, devouring the Metropolitan Temple, the Lincoln school, and the great Emporium. These huge buildings, full of inflammable material, sent great bursts of flame two or three hundred feet into the air. The hot breath of the fire fiend made our roof very uncomfortable for those who were up there. On the west side, a lot of frame buildings made a fierce heat that was hard to stand against, especially since the openings of our roof were bursting into flames from the flying cinders.

With three others I had the pleasure of working for over an hour on this shaky roof, throwing buckets of water on the blazes as they sprang up. At any moment another earthquake might have sent the great chimneys tumbling down on our heads. Three of us refinery men then went down into our department, which is located at the northwest corner of the top floor. Here we knew we would catch it most of all, for the fire was now burning over toward Market Street in the group of structures comprising Hale's, Breuner's, Emma Spreckels and Windsor Hotel buildings. Fanned by a whirlwind of their own making, the flames leaped 200 feet against the north wall of the mint. The roaring was awful as the great buildings crashed and fell, while the bursting of large pieces from our own walls sounded like shells exploding against our mint. We stuck to the windows until they melted, playing a stream of water on the blazing woodwork. Then, as the flames leaped in and the smoke nearly choked us, we were ordered downstairs, for it was supposed that the mint was doomed.

Employees and soldiers stood around the door, nearly strangling, and wondering what chance we would have for our lives if we were driven into the street, where masses of flames bordered either side. Some, who for reasons best known to themselves, did not show up when the mint was in danger, now say we could have escaped if we wanted to. There is not a man of us, whose judgment is worth anything, who does not know that we were prisoners and fighting for our lives, as well as the preservation in good shape of over $300,000,000 in the vaults.

Finally we made our way back through the smoke to the refinery, and with a hose succeeded in putting out the burning interior, where the flames had gotten under lively headway. We then climbed out on to the roof and played the hose on the red hot copper surface over the gold kettles. There we worked for an hour, ripping up sheet copper and playing the water and using the hose where they would do the most good.

At a little before 5 o'clock we were free to go and see what had become of our various homes. The north side of Market Street had not then burned, and after dancing over the hot cobbles of Fifth Street for a block we reached the sheltered side and looked back on the battle-scarred mint.

TREASURY DEPARTMENT,
WASHINGTON, May 1, 1906.

MY DEAR MR. LEACH:—On April 20 I sent you a telegram as follows:

"Accept thanks for your heroic conduct, and that of the men under you. What national banks are there in San Francisco or suburbs in condition to do business? What action by this department would you recommend to relieve the situation? Can you locate Assistant Treasurer Jacobs or his deputy?"

I now write to confirm the same and to say to you and through you to your associates how much the department appreciates the heroic work performed by you and them. It requires courage of the highest rank to defend a single building from within while everything burns on four sides. Again I congratulate you. I also thank you for your telegram of the 21st ultimo, which conveys much interesting information. Very sincerely yours,

(Signed) L. M. SHAW.

Honorable F. A. Leach, Superintendent United States Mint, San Francisco, Cal.

May 15, 1906.

Honorable L. M. Shaw, Secretary of the Treasury, Washington, D. C.:

MY DEAR SIR—I assure you that I greatly appreciate the commendations you have so generously bestowed upon us here at the mint. While the men had a pretty hot time of it, and it was hard to tell which would conquer, the fire or the mint employees, still I am afraid that distance has magnified the achievement of saving the building. Nevertheless, it is most gratifying to know that what was done has given satisfaction and pleasure to you and other officials of the department. It was also very gratifying to us to note that the banking interests showed their appreciation of your prompt and energetic action which did so much to give stability to the financial conditions.

The mint building is a very busy place now, containing, as it does, the "Bank of All Banks," the Assistant Treasurer, cashier's department for the receipt and disbursement of the relief fund, the refinery agency, the mint gold deposit business, and, last but not least, our restaurant, the only one so far for miles.

I have the emergency repairs to the building well along. These repairs consist mainly in replacing the destroyed windows and frames, of which there are over sixty-odd in number. Notwithstanding the large additions to our family, everything is running smoothly, without confusion or rush. Respectfully yours,

FRANK A. LEACH, *Superintendent.*

May 2, 1906.

Mr. F. A. Leach, Superintendent, United States Mint, San Francisco, Cal.:

MY DEAR MR. LEACH—I have just received a letter from Mr. Bert Clark, our representative in San Francisco, in which he mentioned a pleasant visit which he had with you a few days ago.

I have thought of you many times during the past two weeks, and I think I can well imagine the strenuous period you have been passing through. As soon as I learned that the sub-treasury had been destroyed and that the mint was still standing, I realized that you would be the center of an important situation, and I felt confident that you would acquit yourself with credit under the circumstances.

The first really intelligible account of the San Francisco situation which I read was your telegram, sent to Washington, and, upon reading it, I realized more than ever the value of the sort of training which a successful newspaperman receives. I am sure that no other official of the government on the spot could have written so lucidly and briefly, or have expressed so much in a few words.

I sincerely hope that you suffered no serious personal losses in the conflagration and that you will not overwork yourself by trying to straighten things out and keep the treasury business moving. It must be hard, I know, for a person in your responsible position to take any more time for rest than is absolutely necessary, but for many weeks to come you will require the use of all your energy and it will be a great mistake to overdo things now.

With best wishes and sincere regard, I am,
  Cordially yours, (Signed) F. A. VANDERLIP.

May 16, 1906.

Mr. F. A. Vanderlip, National City Bank, New York, N. Y.:

MY DEAR MR. VANDERLIP—Your kind and very complimentary letter of May 2 came duly to hand. However, a very "great stress of business" of unusual character has prevented my acknowledging your kindness before. Your letter was especially appreciated, as it seemed to express something more than was laid down with simply ink and paper.

While the situation imposed increased labor and greater responsibilities, I assure you I enjoyed it, for there was real pleasure in contributing to relief and to the work of organizing and restoring financial conditions. The mint building is a busy place, housing the "Bank of All Banks," the sub-treasury, the cashier's department for the relief fund, office of the Selby company, and our own business. As there were no eating or lodging places for a great distance, I had to provide lodgings in the building for a lot of my own men and start a restaurant for their subsistence and the accommodation of many others in the mint building. We fed over 100 people for a few days, but now the number is considerably less.

The building had a close call from destruction. It was on fire inside of the upper story and roof many times. There is quite a section of the roof that will have to be replaced. During the worst part of the fire around the building, burning embers and red hot cinders rained down upon us in perfect showers, and they would find lodgment against every projection on the roof, and in one place for twenty feet long they accumulated to the depth of about two feet. This was about the time the building was being scarred up as you see it in the picture. The windows there were all burned out, and the boarding up shown in the picture was done the day after the fire. The hose streams we had on the inside of the building and roof enabled us to prevent the fire getting any serious foothold. I had a brave lot of fellows who stood up to the fight while their flesh and clothes were scorched. I did not expect to save the building. It was sufficiently hot to make trouble for us on the south and west sides, and as the buildings on the north side were larger, taller, and nearer, with the wind against us, it appeared to me as if no possible power could protect the building from destruction, but the character of the structure and our fire plant won the day. By the way, the latter was completed only about ten days before the fire.

I am pleased to say my personal loss did not amount to anything worth mentioning. I live in Oakland, where the damage was less than in San Francisco.

The condition of the mint building, which, outside of the chimneys, has not a crack in it, and other first class buildings, shows it is possible to build against damage by earthquakes. A cheap, three-story building, a half block from here on Fifth Street, was thrown completely down.

California can not express its gratitude for the extraordinary showing of generosity on the part of the people of New York and other parts of our country. We have been placed under a debt we never can discharge.

I shall be pleased to be remembered to Mr. Clark.

Again thanking you for the kindly interest manifested, and with full appreciation of the soundness of your advice, I am, Yours truly,

(Signed) FRANK A. LEACH.

UNITED STATES SENATE.
COMMITTEE ON CIVIL SERVICE AND RETRENCHMENT.
WASHINGTON, D. C., April 27, 1906.

Honorable F. A. Leach, Superintendent of the Mint, San Francisco, Cal.:

MY DEAR LEACH—I wish to express to you and to the employees of the mint who worked with you the appreciation of the Secretary of the Treasury and all the officials of the government and of the California delegation of the great work performed by you by which the most important structure in San Francisco was saved from destruction. Had it not been for the efforts of yourself and the employees of the mint, San Francisco would now be in a desperate plight financially, without adequate means for making money transfers, which is of such vital necessity at the present time. I can assure you and all those who risked their lives in the great work that the services performed are appreciated by the government, by Congress, and by all people who have given thought to the various needs of a stricken people. It is no more than just that the government has determined to maintain the pay-roll of the mint and other public offices without change, even should there not be work to fully employ every one, and the delegation will use every effort to promote the interests of all those who have shown themselves to be brave and faithful in time of stress.

I remain, Cordially yours,

(Signed) GEO. C. PERKINS.

TREASURY DEPARTMENT.
OFFICE OF THE DIRECTOR OF THE MINT.
WASHINGTON, April 23, 1906.

DEAR MR. LEACH:—The Bureau of the Mint is living in the light of your glory these days. We are all very proud of the work done by yourself and helpers who saved the mint while fire swept by on all sides. It was a great achievement.

The calamity to San Francisco is almost inconceivable in its magnitude. I can not realize that the splendid business section is absolutely obliterated. But while it means hopeless ruin to thousands, there can be no doubt that the city will rebuild and in a few years be greater than ever. I am wondering if Oakland will not, however, receive a permanent impetus from the transfer of so much business to it temporarily. It has always seemed to me that there was the natural place for the great city.

With personal regards, Very truly yours,

(Signed) GEO. E. ROBERTS,
Director of the Mint.

Frank A. Leach, Esq., Superintendent United States Mint, San Francisco.

TEMPORARY OFFICE 2129 LAGUNA ST.
SAN FRANCISCO CLEARING HOUSE ASSOCIATION.
SAN FRANCISCO, May 8, 1906.

Honorable F. A. Leach, Superintendent United States Mint, San Francisco, Cal.:

DEAR SIR—The following resolution, passed at a meeting of the San Francisco Clearing House Association, May 7, 1906, I trust you will accept as an expression of our high appreciation of your kindness to its members one and all:

"RESOLVED, That the thanks of the San Francisco Clearing House Association, and of the community, be tendered to Honorable Frank A. Leach, Superintendent of the United States mint at San Francisco, for the efficient and courteous manner in which he is carrying out the spirit of the Treasury Department policy, and for the desire he has manifested to serve the city's financial interests to the utmost." Very truly yours,

SAN FRANCISCO CLEARING HOUSE ASSOCIATION.
HOMER S. KING, *President.*

Chapter 3

Directorship of the Mint

IN JULY, 1907, the year following the great fire, George E. Roberts, Director of the Mint at Washington, resigned from the position and the place thus made vacant was tendered me. I accepted the appointment and thus became a bureau chief in the Treasury Department. The acceptance of the office necessitated my resignation of the superintendency of the San Francisco mint. Having entered upon the duties of Superintendent August 1, 1897, and resigned September 19, 1907, I had held the office for a trifle over ten years, which was a longer service by several years than ever before given by one man to the superintendency. I was becoming tired of bearing the very great responsibilities of the office and was thinking seriously of resigning when I received the offer of being made chief of the mint bureau. As the duty of the new position carried no financial responsibilities with it, the appointment afforded the release from those I had longed to shake off. When it became known that I was to resign the San Francisco position, the San Francisco bankers paid me a very great compliment in the shape of a set of resolutions, especially thanking me for services rendered the banking world after the fire, adopted by their association. Tne resolutions were engrossed in mag-

SKETCH by the author of an adobe house still standing near Pleasanton, Alameda County. This is a type of domiciles built in California by the Spanish and Mexicans before the American occupation. They were quite common about the bay section in early days, but now it is a matter of good fortune to find one that through care has escaped the ravages of time or the destructive forces of the elements.

Directorship of the Mint

nificent and most costly form, and presented to me by Homer S. King of the Bank of California, I. Steinhart of the Anglo-California Bank, and Wellington Gregg of the Crocker National Bank. In addition, the association presented me with a library of several hundred volumes of standard works and a very costly watch, bearing on the cover a neat engraving of the San Francisco mint on one side and a monogram of my initials on the other, with my name in full on the inside of the case, coupled with a record of the gift and its source. In acknowledging the testimonials I said that these gifts, bearing such strong messages of good will, kindness, and esteem, with such close connection with one of the greatest tragedies in the world's history, would ever possess historical interest, as well as be most highly cherished by me.

The officers and men of the mint, with whom I had been so long associated, manifested their good feeling toward me with kind words of regret that I was to leave them, and pleasure that I had been promoted to a higher office. A more formal testimonial was the presentation of a fine oil portrait of myself which they caused to be painted and which they hung in the mint building. I received a number of letters and telegrams congratulating me on my promotion from friends and acquaintances, messages that warmed the heart and brightened the world from my point of vision. The unpleasant part of the change was the necessity of having to make Washington my place of residence, leaving behind all the friends of a lifetime and those so dear to us by family ties. The packing up of our belongings for the trip and preparing the old home for use by others in our absence were accompanied by a feeling of sadness, a depression of spirits I could not shake off, for the move meant the breaking up of the old homestead and disruption of the family circle.

We arrived in Washington in time for me to assume my new duties about the first of October. I was received most kindly and welcomed in my official capacity by President Roosevelt, Secretary Cortelyou, and Treasurer Treat. With the Secretary of the Treasury, Mr. Cortelyou, I had enjoyed previous acquaintance, and I found several other friends holding positions in the department, so that I was able to assume the position of Director of the Mint with the feeling that I was not altogether a stranger. In fact, all the officers with whom I came in contact, without exception, treated me with the courtesy and spirit of amity that was very gratifying and went a long way in repressing feelings of strangeness and embarrassment.

Now I will say something about the position and duties I had assumed. As Director I was the chief of the bureau of the mint, which brought all the mints (then four) and all the government assay offices (nine) under my supervision. In a general way the working parts of the bureau embraced three divisions, namely, examining or auditing, statistical, and laboratory. The requirements of the first division brought every expenditure made in the mints and assay office to the bureau for audit, where not only the accuracy, but authority and necessity had to be passed upon, as well as to determine if purchases and expenditures were made with proper observation of laws and rules regarding prices paid. To illustrate the care the government exercises in watching the expenditures of congressional appropriations made by the Treasury Department, I will mention that the Auditor of the Treasury revises all these accounts after the audit of the bureau of the mint. Then afterwards, the Comptroller of the Treasury examines them in search of any irregularity that might have been overlooked by the preceding examination. The investigations of this latter official more particularly related to the legality of expenditures, as simple errors seldom pass the other auditors.

The division of statistics had the work of gathering the figures which showed the annual production of gold

Directorship of the Mint

and silver in the United States and in all other countries of the world, so that at the close of each calendar year an official statement may be given of such statistics. The production reports made by the Director of the Mint of the United States have for many years been accepted by writers on economics, and by officials in all other countries, as standard authority. In this division, record of the kind and quantity of money in use in the United States is kept, and regular statements are made through the Secretary of the Treasury, showing the total and its relation in amount per capita to the population. Much care is exercised in keeping the account, as the statements of this record are also accepted throughout the world as authority by economists and financial writers. Here also is compiled quarterly the table of the value of foreign coins in many of the United States, which table, by act of Congress, is made the standard of value in all custom house transactions and in the courts.

In the laboratory divisions, the principal work is to examine the samples of the coinage as it is made at the different mints, both as to weight and fineness; that is, to find if the coins contain the proper quantity of copper alloy with the gold or silver, within the limitations allowed by law, and also if the proper weights are maintained. That a prompt examination may be made of all coinage, the regulations require from each mint samples of each day's work to be sent to the Director for examination and test. The coinage from which the samples are taken is not released for circulation until the examination has determined the work to have been properly executed. Incidents of imperfect coinage are seldom recorded; nevertheless, the system of inspection is maintained as if it were something of frequent or daily occurrence.

The Director of the Mint has responsibilities outside of the routine mentioned, one of which is to see that the coinage of the mint is of the particular denominations required in the needs of trade and finance, and is promptly met in time and quantity. Ordinarily this obligation is met without trouble or anxiety, but there are times when enlivened conditions of trade exhaust the surplus stock of some particular denomination or denominations of coins in the Treasury of the United States, and the ordinary working capacity of the mints is unable to meet the requirements. This was the condition of things when I assumed the duties of Director in the fall of 1907. The extraordinary expansion of trade which ultimately resulted in a financial panic required the full capacity of the four mints working overtime to meet the demands for silver coins. Never before in the history of our country was so much coin of that character made by the mints in the same space of time. Nothing like it could be found in the records. When in October of that year the panic disrupted business affairs, and factories were shut down and employment contracted, the need for the extra coinage was at an end and the silver and minor coinage not required in trade and for the payment of wages began to flow back into the Treasury of the United States until a surplus of something like $30,000,000 had accumulated. The record of the holdings by the Treasurer of this kind of money acts as an accurate barometer of business conditions in the United States. When trade and commerce are expanding there is an increased employment of labor and more transactions in the stores. For every new hand employed and every additional transaction, there is a draft upon the surplus of the Treasury, and a corresponding increase of the stock of money in circulation. The workingman's pocket, when he is employed, carries money, and is empty when he is unemployed. The storekeeper needs a greater amount of silver, nickels, and coppers for change, when his volume of trade is enlarged. When the number of the storekeeper's business transactions falls off and trade becomes dull, that kind of money

Directorship of the Mint

accumulates on his hands and he deposits the surplus in his bank. The banks, not being able to use the surplus of this kind of money, turn it into the Treasury of the government and receive, in exchange, currency or gold coin. Thus it is seen that with the increase or expansion of trade the surplus or stock of small coin in the Treasury is reduced by drafts upon it. The flow is outward, and when a reverse condition of business takes place then the flow is into the Treasury and the surplus is increased, and the Director of the Mint has only to watch the daily cash statements of the Treasurer, taking into consideration the additions to stock made by the mint operators, to be informed as to the status of business conditions in the country as a whole, and to be advised as to the needs in coinage operations.

Another very important matter was in hand in the bureau when I arrived at Washington, which was soon to cause me some anxiety, and that was the perfection of President Roosevelt's scheme for new designs for all the gold coins of our country. There were a number of prominent people in the East, especially in New York and Boston, who some time before began an agitation for an improvement in appearance of all our coinage. The President quickly became the leading spirit of the movement. The prevalent idea in this undertaking was that the design and execution of our coinage were inferior and inartistic when compared with those of ancient Greece; and as the coins used by a nation are one of the most enduring records of the art and mechanical skill of its age, our government should make an issue of coinage that would leave to future generations and ages something that would more truthfully and correctly reflect the artistic taste and mechanical ability of our day than the coinage then in use, unchanged for so many years. The admiration for the ancient Greek coins unwittingly influenced those gentlemen to suggestions that were imitative rather than original. They wanted the designs for the proposed coinage to be brought out in high relief, or with medallic effect, like the designs on the ancient coins. The commercial use and requirements seemed to have been lost sight of in the enthusiasm of producing a highly artistic coin; but in all probability none of the leading spirits in the movement was familiar with the use of metallic money, and did not understand that the proposed high relief would make the face of the coins so uneven that the pieces would not "stack," which was a condition fatal to the practicability of the idea.

It was early in the year 1905 that President Roosevelt authorized the Director of the Mint to conclude a contract with the famous sculptor, Saint-Gaudens, to supply designs in high relief for the $20 and $10 gold coins. This was accomplished in July, but no designs were finally perfected that met the approval of the President until the early part of 1907. The first model was a design for the double eagle, or $20 piece. Dies from the model were made at the Philadelphia mint. On trial, the dies gave such a high relief to the figures on the design that all efforts to produce a perfect or satisfactory coin on the regular coining presses were ineffectual. A medal press was then resorted to, that the beauty of the design might be studied and be preserved in the shape of a coin, but even by this process it required about twelve blows or impressions in the press for each piece, with an annealing process between each stroke of the process. The annealing process consists of heating the coin to a cherry-red heat and cooling it in a diluted solution of acid. This process eliminates the copper alloy on the surface of the coin and leaves the piece covered with a thin film of pure gold. As a work of art the pieces were beautiful, but had more the appearance of medals than coins for daily use. Nineteen pieces only from this model were struck on the medal press, and these were subsequently given to mint and Washington officials connected with the work.

There were some who thought that by reducing the diameter of the piece to about the size of a "checker," with a corresponding increase in thickness, the much desired high relief might be struck on the ordinary coin press; accordingly dies were made and several pieces struck, when it was discovered that the coinage act, passed in 1890, prohibited the change of the diameter of any coin. Thirteen pieces were struck from this small die for the thick or checker pieces, but with the exception of two coins placed in the cabinet or collection of coins at the Philadelphia mint, all of these pieces were melted and destroyed on account of the improper or illegal dimensions.

Saint-Gaudens then attempted to facilitate the work of coinage by supplying another or second set of models with the relief reduced to some extent, but satisfactory results were not obtained on the regular coinage presses. He then made a third model with still further and greater reduction of the high relief. The failure gave rise to considerable friction between the artist and the mint authorities. The President had become impatient and began to think that the mint officials were not showing a zeal in the work that promised results. It was at this stage of the undertaking that I came into the office of Director. Before I had become familiar with my surroundings the President sent for me. In the interview that followed he told me what he wanted, and what the failures and his disappointments had been, and proceeded to advise me as to what I should do to accomplish the purpose determined upon in the way of the new coinage. In this talk he suggested some details of action of a drastic character for my guidance, which he was positive were necessary to be adopted before success could be had. All this was delivered in his usual vigorous way, emphasizing many points by hammering on the desk with his fist. This was my first interview with the President, and it was somewhat embarrassing for me to oppose his views, but I felt that it was essential to my success that I should be untrammelled by any interference in the plans that I should adopt to secure the production of the new coinage. I determined then and there that if I could not have free rein in the matter I would not attempt the work. In my reply to the President I finally made the wisdom of my position clear to him. I explained to him how I had not yet had time to look into the matter and locate the causes of failure, consequently could not say what was necessary to correct them. At any rate, I would have to insist that these were matters of details that should be left to my judgment.

"All you want, Mr. President," I said, "is the production of the coin with the new design, is it not?"

"Yes," said he.

"Well, that I promise you."

He said he guessed I was right in my attitude in the matter, but I think he was not very confident of my getting results, for when a few days later I laid upon his desk a sample of beautifully executed double eagles of the Saint-Gaudens design, he was most enthusiastic in his expressions of pleasure and satisfaction. I certainly believed him when he declared he was "delighted." He warmly congratulated me on my success, and was most complimentary in his comments.

"Now," said he, "I want enough of these coins within thirty days to make a distribution throughout the country, that the people may see what they are like." I replied that we would be able to meet with his desire, although I explained that this issue would have to be struck on medal presses from the second design model, but that in a few weeks later we would have dies completed from model No. 3 with lower relief, so that the coins, when made, would meet the requirements of the bankers and business men in "stacking," etc., and these could be struck on the regular coin presses in the usual way. The pleasure of the President was manifested in the heartiness of his thanks. I had every medal press in the Philadelphia mint put into operation on these coins with an extra force of workmen, so that the presses were run night and day. The officers of the mint entered into the spirit of the work cut out for them, putting a zest into the operations which assured me that the issue of the new double eagles, so greatly desired by the President, would be made on time. In fact, we delivered to the Treasurer of the United States 12,153 double eagles, representing $243,060, which was considerably more than asked of us, several days ahead of time. I came in for more compliments from the President. In his enthusiastic way he introduced me to several of his Cabinet officers who were present in his office, as a "man who got results." The coins of this issue, when made available to the public, were much sought after by people who wanted to keep them as souvenirs or as additions to numismatic collections. Contrary to expectations, a premium was demanded by dealers soon after the distribution began, and by the time it was ended the premium had increased to about an average of fifteen dollars on a piece. The newspapers gave much space to criticism, both by their own editors and from correspondents. Opinions as to the merits of the new coin were fairly well divided. The artistic appearance of the coin was generally recognized, but it could scarcely claim a popular reception. The design of the eagle on the reverse side of the coin was the object of much adverse comment. Saint-Gaudens did not use any originality in this design of the eagle, but simply copied that used on the penny coined in 1857, following the feature of the bird flying with its talons extended backward under the tail feathers, instead of being drawn up under the breast, the position most generally observed in birds of prey when flying about.

While discussing with the President the criticism by the public, I spoke of the position of the talons as being incorrect. This the President promptly denied, and said that if I would visit the large aviary at Rock Creek Park I would find the eagles flying about just as represented by the Saint-Gaudens design. I did not know then that the President was such a close observer of things in nature, and, having doubts as to the accuracy of his opinion, I went to the aviary as he had suggested. I did not have to wait to be convinced of the correctness of the President's assertion, for the very first flight of an eagle across the aviary showed the talons extended out behind, in the manner of a crane or gull.

The greatest extent of unpleasant criticism over the new issue was aroused by the discovery that the motto, "In God we trust," had been omitted from it. The President's mail, as well as that of the Secretary of the Treasury, was flooded with letters, some mild and many bitter, in protest against the removal of the motto. So loud became this protest that the President felt called upon to defend the omission, in a statement to the press, wherein he took the position that it was a profane use of the name of God, and the motto had been very properly omitted. He could have made an explanation that would have silenced all criticism and relieved himself of the responsibility for the omission if he had referred his critics to coinage acts of the government.

The statutes of the United States supply the only words and mottoes that shall appear on the various coins authorized by the act of Congress. For many years the motto, "In God we trust," was included with other word requirements by law. In 1890 the coinage act was changed in several particulars, and when the re-enactment was completed the motto in question, whether by

Directorship of the Mint

design or accident, had been omitted. So when Saint-Gaudens was given the words and figures that must appear on the coins, the motto was not included. When this was understood an appeal was made to Congress, and that body quickly authorized the restoration of the words, "In God we trust."

While the people were talking about the new coins, the mint officials were busy working on the dies from model number three, and their efforts to produce them on the ordinary coining presses were finally crowned with success, and by the latter part of December the mint presses were striking off new double eagles at the rate of about $1,000,000 daily. Excepting the addition of the motto, the design is the same as that used in the coining of $20 pieces at all the mints of the government ever since.

About the same experience was encountered in producing the $10 pieces, or eagles. Three models of the new design were made by Saint-Gaudens. Five hundred trial pieces were struck from the first model, and 34,100 pieces were struck from the second model, but all of this lot were subsequently remelted except forty-two coins, which, with those of the first lot, were given to museums of art and officials and others connected with the work. Dies from the third model were found to work satisfactorily in the ordinary coining presses.

The new $10 pieces came in for more severe and adverse criticism than the double eagle received. First, for the omission of the motto; next, that the emblem of the eagle was a monstrosity; third, an accusation that the artist had posed his Irish servant girl to secure his design of the Indian maiden's head appearing on the obverse side of the coin. The omission of the motto has been explained. The criticism of the eagle was unjust, and showed unfamiliarity with bird life on the part of the critics. This eagle was copied from one of Audubon's famous drawings. The majority of the people who handled coin probably had never seen a live eagle, and the only idea they had of what the king of birds looked like was formed from the travesty on the bird that has appeared on the coins of the country ever since the mints were established. The President was right in his judgment; if an emblem of freedom was to be used on the coins, good taste demanded the most accurate representation of it, and artists say the Saint-Gaudens design was a truthful copy from nature. The third feature of complaint was groundless. No Irish servant girl, or any other girl, had posed for Saint-Gaudens for the head design of the Indian maiden. Saint-Gaudens copied the design from the experimental penny of 1857, the same coin from which he obtained the idea of the flying eagle used on the new double eagle. It is a most excellent copy, as any one will find who will take the trouble to compare the two coins, the old cent of 1857, and the new $10 piece. The designs and appearance of the new coin, however, were not beyond criticism. In my judgment the artist unduly lengthened the legs of the eagle to better center the design on the piece. It was but a trifle, but it was enough to cause some critics to make fun of the bird. The more serious fault was on the obverse side. When it was decided to adopt an Indian head design an accurate representation of a real Indian, head dress, and ornaments, should have been selected for the purpose, for the same reason manifested in the selection of the emblem of the eagle. Such designs should not be ideal or imaginary. If worth using, they should be faithful to the subject represented. The original design of the Indian maiden copied by Mr. Saint-Gaudens was made more than fifty years before, evidently by some one who had a very imperfect conception of what a real Indian looked like. Apparently the original artist's opportunity for the knowledge had not extended beyond the old pictures of "Columbus Discovering America."

Directorship of the Mint

Originally it was the intention to give the $5 and $2.50 pieces the same design as that used on the double eagle or $20 piece, but before final action to that end was taken President Roosevelt invited me to lunch with him at the White House. His purpose was to have me meet Doctor William Sturgis Bigelow of Boston, a lover of art and friend of the President, who was showing great interest in the undertaking for improving the appearance of American coins, and who had a new design for the smaller gold coins. It was his idea that the commercial needs of the country required coins that would "stack" evenly, and that the preservation of as much as possible of the flat plane of the piece was desirable. A coin, therefore, with the lines of the design, figures, and letters depressed or incused, instead of being raised or in relief, would meet the wishes of the bankers and business men, and at the same time introduce a novelty in coinage that was artistic as well as adaptable to the needs of business. The President adhered to the idea that the high relief afforded greater possibilities of artistic results, and referred to the beauties of the ancient gold coins. Unquestionably he was correct in this opinion, but I called his attention to the fact that he and the other promoters of the new coinage were trying to do more than the ancient Greek artists and coiners had found possible, and that the Greeks had only been able to produce a high relief on one side of their coins, while we were endeavoring to give a high relief on both sides. We had in a way succeeded, for by the use of a medal press we had outdone the Greeks. But the uncompromising demands of trade would not tolerate even the one-sided coins of ancient Greece. The President expressed surprise at my statement, and at once sent a messenger to his room for a beautiful example of Grecian work in the shape of a gold coin of the days of Alexander the Great. Of course, he found one side quite flat, while the other was in high relief.

I enjoyed the luncheon. It was as simple and devoid of ceremony as a lunch would be in the home of any well-to-do family. Mrs. Roosevelt, a lady friend, and a federal judge, an old-time friend of the President, were also at the table. It so happened that it was the anniversary day of April, 1865, of the surrender of the judge as a Confederate army officer in the closing days of the Civil War. As might be imagined, it put the judge in a reminiscent mood. He was an excellent talker and interested us all. One of his remarks was that no one could tell what would happen in life. "The day I surrendered as a Confederate soldier I little expected to stretch my legs under a dining table in the White House, as a guest of the President. Why, I remember I was so dejected on that occasion that an aged friend of mine said to me, 'You think you and the country are going to hell on a toboggan, but that is all wrong.' So I found out."

It was after the lunch and we had excused ourselves from the others that the question as to the new design for the half and quarter eagles took place. The discussion ended by the President authorizing Doctor Bigelow and me to go ahead and produce some trial pieces after the suggestions of the doctor. Bela L. Pratt, an artist of high repute in Boston, was selected to make the models for the designs, which were to be a faithful copy of an Indian head and the eagle with shortened legs. The models and dies were not finished until some time in September. When the trial pieces were produced I was pleased with their appearance, for the nationality was so plainly stamped on the coin that it needed no lettering to tell anybody in any part of the world that it had been issued by the United States of America. It pleased the President, and he at once gave the official approval necessary for the adoption of the design. Soon after, the new coins were minted and placed within the reach of the public. Considerable criticism followed the appearance of the

Directorship of the Mint

new design. The depressed or incused idea of portraying the figures, device, etc., was unfavorably received, while the faithfulness of the designs to the objects represented, as artistic work, was very generally commended. Confirming the truth of the old saying, "there is nothing new in the world," we found, in looking over some authorities on ancient coinage, that almost the very first attempt in making coins was by depressing or incusing the designs. This issue finished the work of changing the designs of the gold coins.

Without the authority of Congress, the coinage laws of our country permit the change of designs on any denomination of our coins only once in twenty-five years. For this reason, the only other denominations that could undergo a change of designs were the nickels and copper cent pieces.

Congress passed an act early in the year of 1908 restoring the motto, "In God We Trust," so that all coins made thereafter bore these words.

In 1905, when President Roosevelt conceived the idea of changing the design of the several coins of our country, the cent was one of the denominations selected for alteration and improvement, and the work of making the new design was turned over to Saint-Gaudens at the time he was given the contract for changing the designs of the gold coins. His first work, after completing the design for the double eagle, was making the models for the cent. He made a model of a female head, adorned with an Indian feather head dress, much the same in general appearance as the head in use on the coin at that time. When this model was presented to the President for his consideration, he decided to adopt it as the obverse side for the new $10 gold piece. This changed the original plan of having the eagle, half eagle, and quarter eagle made with the same design as that adopted for the double eage; and as the famous artist was feeble in health, all the time he was able to devote to the work of changing the designs was given to perfecting the models for both the double eagle and eagle for practical mint operations, and the last artistic work of the great man was to beautify the American coins. He finally passed away without making a new design for the cent piece.

Victor D. Brenner of New York, one of the most skillful medalists of this country, was presented to the President with the request that he be given the commission to complete the work the President had in mind of changing the design of the cent piece. As an outcome of this visit, Mr. Brenner was requested by the President to consult with me in the matter. We had several interviews, and upon conclusion I instructed him, with the approval of Secretary Cortelyou, to prepare a model for the obverse side, bearing a portrait of Lincoln. He was also advised as to the law that should be followed in making the design for the reverse side. In due course of time, Mr. Brenner presented the models in accordance with these instructions, which met with the hearty approval of President Roosevelt and Secretary Cortelyou, and were formally adopted as the design for the new cent.

The fact that this change had been decided upon was given considerable publicity in the newspapers at the time, creating a very great interest in the public mind, and the appearance of the new coin was anxiously awaited. The Treasury Department was for a time almost overwhelmed with applications for a supply of the new issue, coming from every part of the United States, but the new coppers were not given to the public until the early part of 1909.

There was some little criticism emanating from those who feared that the use of the head of the ex-President might establish a precedent which would lead ultimately to the adoption of the use of the portraits of existing

Directorship of the Mint

executives on our coins, after the manner of monarchial governments. In this connection it may be of interest to cite the fact that the legislative act establishing the first mint of the United States and providing for a coinage system originated in the Senate. When the bill was sent to the House it contained the provision that the head or portrait of the President should appear on all coins executed during the term of the official, with the numerical order of the presidency. When this act was considered in the House no alteration of the bill was made except to strike out this clause and substitute the following: "An impression emblematic of liberty, and an inscription of the word 'liberty' and the year of the coinage." What was intended in the law by the vague expression of "An impression emblematic of liberty" has been generally interpreted through all these years by the use of a female head, sometimes adorned with the cap of Liberty, and at other times with an Indian head dress, but more frequently without any ornamentation other than a band above the brow holding the hair, bearing the word, "Liberty." Some years ago this matter was made the subject of debate in the Senate, when Senator Morrill of Vermont said:

The emblem of Liberty, like that of many other virtues, has been said to be always represented in petticoats. The Britannia of Great Britain appears in form like a near relation to the Liberty, or the Minerva, often found on old Greek and Roman coins, and in the days of Charles II, the Duchess of Richmond served as a model to the engraver; but, more recently, Victoria, by the distinguished medalist Wyon, has been stamped with great excellence upon British coins, and she, like Queen Anne, seems to have occasionally insisted upon decent drapery about the bust.

Our sitting emblem of Liberty on the fractional silver looks very like a descendant of our grandmother Britannia by Clark Mills. Whether she wears long hair or a widow's cap may not be quite clear, and there is no end of crinoline, while the obtruding whalebones, in bas relief compressing the waist, painfully disclose overworn corsets. But, as our highest effort and best, on the copper cent and on the one-dollar and three-dollar gold coins, the head of our emblem appears in the baubles of an Indian princess, doubtless an ideal Pocahontas—"that female bully of the town"—with the head accordingly stuck around with feathers, and labeled on the tiara, "Liberty." Its circulation in the Indian territory, I regret to say, has not been commensurate to the witchery of the bait. England strangely omits to stamp on her figure of the lion, "This is a lion"; but our emblem, safe from all misconception, is always plainly and veraciously branded across the forehead, "Liberty."

The use of the liberty cap, which appears on some of the earliest coins of our country, was the subject of much discussion as to its appropriateness at periods from 1793, when it was first used, up to some time in the '30s, when it was discarded. Its first use was on the cent pieces of 1794, 1795, and a part of the year 1796, where it appears on the coin as if suspended in the air over the head of a female figure with flowing hair. It was not intended that this cap should appear as suspended in the air, but as being borne on a wand leaning on the shoulder of the figure and projecting backward. It was contended that the liberty cap, or pileus, was in itself an emblem of liberty and should never be placed on the head of the figure; and that the emblem in proper relation to a full-length figure of Liberty should be borne on a wand or staff sustained in her hand and was out of place as an adornment or head dress.

During the time that I filled the office of Director of the Mint nothing was done in the way of preparing a new design for the nickels or five-cent pieces. I had conceived some designs which I thought if adopted for the silver coins would greatly improve their appearance. It was my intention to have some sample coins made, using the head of Washington, copied from the famous Stuart portrait, for the obverse side, and an eagle in natural

Directorship of the Mint

position, standing on the American shield with wings partly spread, making a pose suggestive of courage, freedom, and action. It was my intention to submit the samples to the President and if they met with his approval it was then the further purpose to lay them before Congress, with the hope of securing action that would have permitted the device to take the place of the meaningless designs now used to designate the different silver coins of our country. Some work was done on the proposed models at the Philadelphia mint, but as I had retired from the service before the models were completed, and as Roosevelt had stepped out of office that Taft might take up the responsibilities of the presidency, there was no one in official position interested in the subject sufficiently to complete the work or carry out the suggestion.

IMPORTANT TRANSPORTATION OF COIN

When I left the San Francisco mint there was stored there in the several vaults of the institution the immense sum of two hundred and seventy millions of dollars in gold coin and sixty-one millions of dollars in silver coin, or over three hundred millions of dollars altogether. The gold had been accumulating there for six or seven years or more, after the adoption of the plan of paying people who sold their gold to the mint with checks drawn on the New York sub-treasury. The mint was not well equipped with vaults, as it had not been contemplated that it would ever become one of the storage places for Uncle Sam's surplus cash. Consequently the capacity of the vaults for storage purposes was limited, besides which the vaults were not substantial enough for the purpose and did not give that security demanded for government funds. The possibility that some bold and desperate men would attempt to secure some of this gold, either by tunnelling under the building or rushing the place during working hours, was always a source of anxiety to me. Especially was this so after overhearing in a theater one evening a couple of fellows who sat to the rear of me discussing the matter and expressing the opinion that a great theft in some such manner could be successfully carried out. Besides, there was another strong reason for its removal. In case of war, being so handy and easy of access, the vast sum might fall into the hands of an enemy as a result of some brief or temporary advantage.

At the new Denver mint there had been constructed a fine large and strong vault with the most modern devices for security. It was located far inland from any seacoast, consequently any treasure stored there was comparatively secure from capture by foreign invaders. Here, then, was the place to which the gold and silver at the San Francisco mint should be transferred; but in its transfer it would be subject to dangers of loss by theft in the handling in a petty way and robbery on a large scale by train robbers. I laid the matter before the Secretary of the Treasury, Mr. Cortelyou. He asked me to make a statement of the facts so that the subject could be presented to the President, as he considered it of great importance and something that should have immediate attention. A decision in accordance with my views and recommendations was quickly reached, but we were confronted with the fact that there was no money with which to defray the expense of the transfer. There was nothing to do but to appeal to Congress for the money, with the hope that the appropriation might be made without undue publicity of its precise purpose. It was our intention to make the transfer, if possible, without knowledge of the fact being made public while the coin was being transferred, and in this way reduce to the minimum the danger of loss of money and conflict with robbers. The Secretary sent for the chairman of the Committee on Ways and Means of the House, **Mr. Tawney,** and explained the situation and asked him to secure the appropriation of the sum I had asked for, $300,000. Mr. Tawney handled the matter very cleverly, for none of the facts stated to him ever became public, and no newspaper mention of the appropriation appeared. The sum mentioned was quickly made available, and as soon as possible I was on the way to San Francisco with full authority to make arrangements for the transfer of the largest sum of metallic money ever made. It was quite a matter to arrange the details for moving several carloads of gold, but to arrange for the transfer without publication of such an extraordinary event was quite another matter and caused many anxieties. Arrangements with the express company had to be made, and the United States Marshal had to be authorized to employ thirty guards. Then there were the workmen, handling, packing, and storing, employed at both ends of the route, to add to the sources through which knowledge of the transfers might be made public.

Finally the bargain with Wells Fargo & Co. was completed and all other details were finished, and I was able to start the first shipment of gold to Denver on August 15, 1908. Thereafter two shipments of $5,000,000 each per week were made. The money was placed in horse-cars and made a part of the regular express trains. As horse-cars were common in express trains, they did not attract any more attention when filled with millions of dollars in gold coin than when occupied by fancy race horses. Each shipment was accompanied by fifteen deputy United States marshals in citizens' clothes. These were all tried and trusted men, selected with the greatest care by Captain Seymour, formerly Chief of Detectives in San Francisco.

At the San Francisco mint a force was organized to handle the gold. These men were all skilled in that kind of work and were exceedingly trustworthy. The plan of operation was to take the gold out of the vault and weigh it, which was the usual manner of determining the value of gold. It was stored in the mint in canvas sacks holding $5000 each. It was weighed in the sacks, one of which was occasionally opened to show that its contents were really what they were supposed to be. Then the sacks were packed in strong pine boxes, bound with iron bands, $40,000 to each box, weighing about 140 pounds. The lids of the boxes were screwed on and then the boxes were sealed with the seal of the United States by a specially detailed official.

It took one expert weigher and two tally clerks to tally the gold out of the storage vault into the one where the work was done, and two more to keep track of the bags and boxes. There was also a force of laboring men to move the money from vault to vault.

It was figured that by moving two shipments each week there would be only $10,000,000 on the road at any one time. As one shipment reached Denver the next one was just leaving San Francisco. The frequent handling of silver for the Philippine coinage made people familiar with such operations at the mint, and when the express company's wagons backed up twice a week and loaded up ten tons of gold for each shipment but little attention by outsiders was paid to it. Three trucks handled $5,000,000 without any trouble, and there was only the usual complement of two guards to each wagon or truck. It is possible that even they did not know what a fortune they handled at every trip.

The shipments began August 15. When December came they were going forward with great regularity twice a week. Then it was found that, by increasing the shipments to $7,500,000 each time, the work could be completed before the new year, so this was done and the shipments ended on December 19.

Not a dollar was lost, and there was never any sign or rumor of trouble, and not a word appeared in the

Directorship of the Mint

newspapers of San Francisco or Denver giving publicity to the shipments. When the transfer was completed so successfully it added much to the pleasure of reporting the accomplishment to Secretary Cortelyou, and earned from him a very handsome compliment.

AN EX-SENATOR SWINDLED

The office of the Director of Mint was a bureau of information on matters of coinage, past and future, domestic and foreign, as well as in statistics pertaining to productions of precious metals at home and elsewhere. This fact brought many distinguished people to the mint bureau, and in this way I made the acquaintance of a number of the most active Senators and Congressmen of those years, and some prominent writers on economic subjects. I enjoyed this privilege for the opportunity it gave to study the personalities and the character of men of whom all that I had heretofore known were the impressions gained by reading of their activities in public life as presented in newspapers and magazines. One thing that I noticed in sizing up these men from my own observations, and comparing the conclusions with impressions conveyed by the press, was the universal custom of the latter to harp upon and magnify individual peculiarities, making such people in some instances better known to the public by a peculiar trait in habit or appearance than they would otherwise be.

An occasional visitor to my office was an ex-Senator from one of the Pacific Coast states. He was always welcomed, as he was a good talker and gave me many interesting details of stirring political events of the reconstruction work after the close of the Civil War. Finally his visits developed a bold swindle, in which he and two other prominent professional men of Washington were the victims. The Senator came into my office one morning and placed in my hands a lump of gold worth about

$50, requesting me to have it assayed for him. He came back the next morning, when I reported the value and fineness of the lump. After asking me if I was certain of the findings and being told there could be no mistake about it, he went away. A week or so later he came back with a larger lump of gold, which he again asked to have assayed, saying that the importance of having a reliable assay was the reason for bringing it to the mint bureau for determination of its value. The next day I was able to report to the Senator that the value of the gold was practically $1500. In response to his request to know how to sell the gold to the government, I gave him directions how to send the metal to the Philadelphia mint and how he would receive the value in money in return. It was something like ten days later when, early one morning, the Senator came into the office laboring under a state of excitement he could not hide. He asked me to close the doors of the office so that we could have the utmost privacy. Then he declared that he was almost sure that the lump of bullion which he had sold to the Philadelphia mint was not gold and only something in imitation, and he wanted to refund the money he had received before the mint authorities discovered the fraud and caused his arrest. Upon making this declaration he placed a roll of bills on my desk. I assured him that he was certainly mistaken in his opinion of the bullion; for, laying aside our assays, the treatment of deposits at the mints was such as to make it impossible for any one to impose counterfeit bullion on the gold-buying agents of the government. "Now," I said, "come, tell me what has happened." He then went on to relate how a fine-looking man, educated in chemistry and metallurgy, introduced himself some eight or ten weeks before, and, after reading a magazine article relating the wonderful feat of Sir William Ramsay, the famous English chemist, in transmuting a small amount of metallic copper into

Directorship of the Mint

lithium, said what was claimed by Ramsay was not only true, but that he, the stranger, was able to do even more, as he could change silver into gold, and offered to demonstrate the truth of his claim. He was so plausible that the Senator asked to see a demonstration. At the man's house he found a lot of chemical and metallurgical devices arrayed in an impressive manner around the place. The stranger, after allowing the Senator to inspect them, placed a couple of silver dollars in a small cell or tank containing some kind of liquid, then for an hour or so he entertained the Senator in conversation to pass the time necessary for the solution to play its part in the transmutation of the silver dollars into gold. Finally the alchemist drew off the solution, and in the bottom of the cell was remaining some finely divided or powdery stuff, brown in color. This was declared to be the gold resulting from the change. It was carefully gathered, dried, and melted, becoming the $50 lump of gold which he had shown on the occasion of his first visit to my office on this business. The Senator admitted to me that the demonstration surprised him as well as later convinced him that there were merits in the stranger's claim when I reported to him that the lump was real gold. The stranger then offered to make a demonstration on a larger scale if the Senator would supply the silver. To the proposition the Senator agreed, and supplied seventy-five dollar pieces for the purpose. The operation or transmutation occupied the best part of a day and resulted in the larger lump of what is, in mint terms. called a "king," which the Senator sold to the Philadelphia mint for $1500. Now all doubt as to the stranger's ability to transmute silver into gold was removed. The Senator became excited in contemplating the effect of the discovery in the financial world and on civilization throughout the world, so he sought a couple of near friends, a physician and an attorney, feeling that he needed the advantage of support and consultation in a matter of such tremendous import. Now the alchemist was desirous of operating on a still larger scale if his associates would supply about 2500 silver dollars. The offer was accepted. The three watched the proceedings with interest and saw their silver go into a tank filled with solution. This was on a Friday. The tank was locked and the keys given to the Senator, and accepted by him with a confidence of commanding the security of the precious metal in the tank inconsistent in a "man of the world" and in a person who was familiar with all kinds of confidence games and tricks of sharpers. The alchemist said that the process of changing so large an amount of silver into gold could not be completed until the following Monday. In the meantime, as he was out of a supply of certain chemicals that could only be obtained in New York, he would make a trip to that city and return on Monday and complete the operation. Up to Sunday the trio had looked upon the transaction with every expectation of receiving nearly $50,000 in gold for their $2500 in silver. However, on that afternoon they received a telegram from the alchemist, saying that he would not be able to return to Washington as soon as he had expected and warning his partners not to unlock the tank or tamper with the solution, as such an act would not only interrupt the process of transmutation, but cause a loss of the silver in solution. They began to fear that they had been victimized, and therefore immediately proceeded to the laboratory and unlocked and examined the tanks, which they found to contain nothing more or less than water from the Potomac River. Then it was that the Senator had visions of having swindled the Philadelphia mint and having incurred the wrath of the government, which prompted the early visit to my office on the following Monday morning. The trio quietly pocketed their losses and thanked their good luck that the sharper did not propose a

Directorship of the Mint

"transmutation" affecting their pockets on a larger scale. Their only fear was publicity of having been "taken in" on such a simple scheme.

During my connection with the Treasury Department in the two years at Washington I was occasionally called upon to act in matters other than those belonging to the mint bureau. In the fall of 1908 the Secretary of the Treasury, Mr. Cortelyou, and his three assistants left Washington to go to their former residences to cast their votes for Presidential Electors, and President Roosevelt appointed me acting Secretary of the Treasury for the several days of their absence. I treasure the commission issued to me by the President for this service as an expression of his good will and the confidence with which he regarded me as a member of his political family. Nothing occurred during the few days of my administration outside of routine matters, so I am unable to recount any incident giving special importance to the temporary elevation of my duties. The newspapers spoke kindly of the appointment, but referred to it as being unusual, if not unprecedented.

When the matter of selecting the site for the new subtreasury building in San Francisco came up for final decision, Secretary Cortelyou submitted all the formal offers of sites, giving price and locations to me, with a request for my opinion as to which was the most desirable. This seemed to be a small matter at first, but months passed before I was finally through with it. The work necessitated a trip to San Francisco and much correspondence and many interviews with people posted on San Francisco real estate values. After a careful consideration of all the offers, the block between Sansome and Battery, Clay and Merchant streets, considering the price and location, was decided upon as the most desirable. Supervising Architect Taylor also reached the same conclusion, and upon our reports the Secretary concluded to accept the offer for this site. Almost at the moment this conclusion was reached the Secretary received a telegram from the agents of the owners of the corner of Pine and Sansome streets, offering that fine lot as a site at a very reasonable price. The Secretary asked me what I thought about it. In reply, I said that the lot presented in the new offer was more desirable than any of the sites offered in the original proposals, and in fact it was about the best place in the city for the proposed building. The agents came to Washington and the deal was made after some little dickering. Since then, a substantial and costly banking building has been erected by the government. The owners wanted more money than Congress had appropriated for the purchase of a lot, but as the piece of land was larger than was needed by the government, they reserved a piece off the west end of the lot and gave the balance to Uncle Sam for $375,000. This southwest corner of the intersection of Pine and Sansome streets was owned by my father in the very early part of the '50s. He told me that at the time of his ownership there was quite a sand hill just back of the lot. He said that he soon sold the lot for a few hundred dollars, being satisfied with a small gain.

The President, learning of my experience in the printing and publishing business, placed in my hands a great mass of typewritten matter relative to the conduct of the Government Printing Office at the national capital, with the request that I examine it and give him my conclusions. The papers embraced complaints from various departments, answers, reports and sub-reports of investigators, statements of employees and officials of the big print shop, as well as of experts and dealers in paper, printing machinery, furniture, etc. I devoted every moment of the day that I could spare at my office to this task, then took the papers home with me at the close of the day and worked late into the nights for nearly two

Directorship of the Mint

weeks, before I was able to make a report to the President. The charge against the administration of the government printing establishment was extravagant management, making the cost of printing for all the departments exceed the allowance of Congress for blanks, stationery, printing, etc. It was while engaged with this matter that I first met and had acquaintance with Senator Root, the famous Secretary of State of the Roosevelt administration. I found him a very pleasant man to meet. I regarded Mr. Root as the brainiest man, the most practical, and best posted on every-day affairs in Washington official life. I heard President Roosevelt say: "Mr. Root was one of the great Secretaries of State, and we have had some great men in that office." I learned afterwards that the Secretary of the Navy, Victor Metcalf, who, as you know, was from Oakland and an old friend of mine, was responsible for acquainting the President with my knowledge and experience in the printing business. While there was some labor attached to the commission, I rather enjoyed the work and did not object to it.

I regretted the close of President Roosevelt's term of office. I found him a very pleasant man to work with, appreciative of all efforts, and enthusiastically grateful for success in what he considered of public need or utility. I was frequently surprised with exhibitions of his wonderful memory as shown in his dealings with details of affairs and his knowledge of the character and capacity of men. His capacity for work was tremendous. By his systematic methods he was to be found at places in his office and the White House at various hours, as if his activities and official life were being regulated by a time card. Interviews with the President by others than those whose position and official business gave them greater privileges were made by appointments previously arranged. The parties to these appointments would assemble in the Cabinet room adjoining the President's private office, separated by folding doors which remained closed until the hour of the meetings, which as I recall was 11 A. M. By this time the room would be filled with twenty to thirty visitors. Very punctually the doors would be opened and the President would step into the Cabinet room, the visitors would rise and remain standing while he passed around among them, picking out with unerring certainty the visitors present with no purpose other than to gratify an ambition and to be able to say that they had met and talked with the Chief Magistrate when they were in Washington. Notwithstanding, if any of them had prepared speeches they intended to make to the President when presented to him, he did most if not all of the talking, skilfully parrying all attempt at reply. Visitors who had no business seldom obtained more than a few seconds of the President's time, but his humor, good-natured remarks, and manner always placed them in a way of leaving the White House office pleased with the President if not with themselves. When the President, passing from one to another of the visitors, met a person with business, the matter was discussed then and there, if it embraced something that could be disposed of without consumption of more than a few moments of time. He lost not a second of time in the visitors' hour ceremony, for while in the process of sifting out those with no business and ridding himself of those with business of minor importance, his eye would light on those who had more important affairs, and he would signal them to remain or go into his private office to meet him after he had completed the round of the room, which seldom required more than fifteen or twenty minutes. Being occasionally called to the President's office, I was several times a witness to the interesting scene or ceremony described. There was, however, one occasion when the President laid aside for a time the rushing manner, high-pressure action, and the "don't-take-an-unneces-

Directorship of the Mint

sary-second-of-my-time" look, and that was on March 3, 1909, the last day of his term of office, when he received the officials of his administration who called to speak of their regrets at the parting and to bid him good-bye. He stood there, plainly showing the relief he felt in freedom from the cares of the great office he was about to lay aside. His work as President was done. That it had been well done was vouchsafed by the laudations of his countrymen and by the plaudits of the rest of the civilized world. During the seven years of his incumbency in the great office he had made a name for advocating everything that stood for good in government and for the betterment of man, and a name inseparable from the history of our country. On that day he was filled with the spirit that becomes a man conscious of having successfully performed a difficult task, but with it there was tenderness and sincerity of manner never to be forgotten in the farewells to his associates. For myself, I was pleased and proud that I had been even for a short period, and in a very small way, a part of his administration, and it was gratifying to receive his thanks and appreciation for what little assistance I had been able to give him.

I saw considerable of President Taft, who succeeded Roosevelt. He was a very able man and, as everybody knows, of excessively good nature, with a strong ambition to give an administration of his duties that would commend itself to all factions of his party, and at the same time receive the sanction of his countrymen regardless of party organization. His great size, with an increasing avoirdupois, was a matter of considerable annoyance to him. On one occasion, when arranging with him to pose for a likeness from which to make the usual presidential medal, he said to me: "The best photograph I ever had taken was out in your town, and it is the one my wife calls *her* picture." I asked him in what particular did the San Francisco photographer excel. "Oh, he was able to conceal some of my avoirdupois," he replied with a smile. President Taft was broad-minded and had little patience for the small things that divided men, and it was largely due to his efforts to ignore these matters that bred the factions in the Republican party that made his re-election to the presidency an impossibility. His ways of meeting people and his indifference to precedence or system in this matter were most distressing and discouraging to his subordinates whose duty it was to arrange meetings and make appointments for visitors, official and ordinary. Senators were shocked and offended by having the President absorb their time and apparently ignore their presence in his attentions to ordinary visitors. High officials with important affairs in hand, or what they might think to be so, could impatiently wait the President's pleasure by standing first on one foot and then the other, while he with leisurely manner was laughingly engaged in conversation with some other person. It was my good fortune to be present at one of President Taft's first morning hours to visitors, with some other officials familiar with the customs and manner of his predecessor at this hour, and we could not help noting this difference. Taft spent almost as much time with the first visitor he spoke to as Roosevelt did in clearing the room of visitors. Those who had business shook their heads in displeasure, while tourists, of course, were pleased to be able to have something more than a snapshot view of the chief magistrate, and were delighted to be able to carry on some little conversation with him. Whether following private secretaries succeeded in changing the new President's way of meeting these engagements, I have never heard. I left Washington shortly after Mr. Taft's inauguration. With the change of administration, Franklin MacVeagh succeeded Mr. Cortelyou as Secretary of the Treasury. Being the chief of our department, I soon became acquainted with him,

Directorship of the Mint

through the frequency of official interviews. It is a pleasure to say that he was a most capable man and an ideal selection for this important office. He had himself achieved great success in business and was an authority on banking matters, being a finely educated man and, beyond all, practical. He did much by his untiring efforts for new legislation on the currency question, and he accomplished more than was ever done before in stopping wastes in the general cost of running the government. He insisted upon the application of business methods in transacting the government's business, and in this way he succeeded in saving several millions of dollars per year in ordinary expenditures. If the American people appreciate the efforts of their officials in economical administration, his reputation will pass into the history of our country as excelling all others in this direction.

George E. Roberts, a newspaperman of Iowa, who became the Director of the Mint not long after I entered the mint service, and who had served up to the time that I entered upon the duties of Director, early won a place in my heart on account of his kindly ways and generous consideration for those under his direction in the mint work. Besides, to know him was to be impressed with his intelligent ideas on all matters concerning our government and policies of administration, and economic questions in general. He was especially well informed on matters of finance, and moreover possessed a remarkable ability to write on the subject in a way to attract, interest, and instruct the ordinary reader. He had the rare power of stripping financial subjects of dryness and laying them before the people so that all who could read could understand them. He did more than any one writer in the United States to expose the fallacy carried in the silver craze that swept over our country in 1896. To his efforts, more than any other person, belongs the credit of starting the agitation for a reform of our financial system which finally resulted in the new Federal Reserve Bank Act. It was his trenchant pen that first pointed out in language that could be understood, that it was in the power of Congress to prevent the possibility of recurring financial panics by creating a financial system similar to the method common to every other civilized government of the world; that under our money system panics were not the outgrowth of poor business conditions, but were more the results of periods of prosperity. Mr. Roberts has contributed many valuable papers on economic questions to magazines and newspapers.

In Washington, where rules of social life are so rigid and the performance of certain social obligations are so exacting, a person who has hitherto lived a rather unconventional life may be expected to be somewhat disturbed, and view what is required of him as a duty somewhat undesirable, if not disagreeable. I confess that this was my impression, although I was pleased to be able to attend two or three of the President's receptions. I had heard much of the magnificence of these affairs. I had considerable desire, if not curiosity, to be present at an assembly where the foremost ladies and gentlemen of our country had been gathered for social pleasures. These functions were regularly held each winter and were the principal events in Washington social life. They have been so frequently and minutely described that I will not attempt to give an account of my observations. It is, perhaps, needless to add that I avoided all perfunctory social affairs other than those to which my official position required attendance. An amusing incident occurred at an afternoon reception, given by a prominent banker of the city, which Mrs. Leach and I attended not very long after we had taken up our home in Washington. There was no attempt in this affair to make a lavish display of wealth and there was more of a cordial and hospitable atmosphere than is usual in such functions.

Directorship of the Mint

Quite a number of prominent people were there, among whom were several representatives of foreign countries. The host, after introducing me to several of the visitors, finally escorted me to a seat by the side of a lady from New York State, to whom I was introduced with quite an elaborate mention of the official title of my position with the government. The lady was a trifle hard of hearing. The noise of the music and buzzing of conversation probably increased the difficulty of understanding distinctly what the host had said, for she misunderstood him and thought he had described me as an ambassador of some foreign country, the name of which she did not catch. Now this lady was one of thousands who come to Washington as sightseers and who esteem it a matter of great fortune to be able to talk with men prominent in the world, so that they can go back home and interest their friends with tales of association with what in Europe might be called the royalty of the country. I immediately discovered the lady's error and the love of humor prevented me from doing the courteous thing at once in correcting her. She commenced a series of rapid-fire questions leading to information concerning the country I represented. She was particularly anxious, and therefore I presumed she wanted to know just who I was so as to be able to decide whether I was worth while wasting any time on when there might be others of greater importance. She was too proud to confess a deficiency in hearing as an excuse for asking me what country I was from, and too polite to put the question direct. She wanted to know if Washington life differed from what I expected. I replied that I did not recall forming any thought upon the subject, but I could say that I found some difference in the way people observed social customs in Washington and my country.

Next, how long had I enjoyed service of my country in the national capital? I truthfully replied, "Only for a few weeks."

So far I am sure my replies to her queries confirmed her in the belief that she almost had in her hands a live foreigner of distinction; and she did not conceal the pleasure it gave her. Now she wanted to know what kind of weather we had in my country, and if we had snow, and other questions as to climate. So I told her that people who were able to pay for it could in almost any month of the year have any kind of climate they desired. Six months of the year there was scarcely a fleck in the sky, and while on part of our land the sun beat down with almost tropical fierceness, yet such places were in sight of districts of most delightful temperature, as well as mountain sections, marked by the gleaming white of perpetual snow. In truth our climate was unsurpassed by that of any other country on the face of the globe. It was where living out of doors a greater part of the year was a delightful pleasure. My lady friend was plainly perplexed. Her questioning gave me opportunity to speak of our magnificent trees, the palms, magnolias, the grand oaks, the lofty conifera of such great growth that one tree would make lumber sufficient to build a family house. Then I described the wonderful variety of wild flowers and their beauty, growing in such profusion in their season that they colored the landscape and were visible miles away. Our land was rich in varied productive qualities, and I knew of no place on earth that could surpass my country in the variety and excellence of the fruits from its plantations of pineapples and orange groves, its peach and apple orchards, and vineyards, etc. My lady's brow contracted; perhaps the mention of pineapples, palms, and magnolias gave a hint of a possible Oriental origin for me. However, she brought the conversation to a climax by the query if in my country it was lawful for men to have more than one wife. I was cornered, whether it was intentional on her part or not. I was pleased that it was so, for it was with difficulty I had held my composure, and I felt I had gone further than proprieties should permit. Therefore I said: "My dear lady, you have evidently been laboring under a mistaken idea as to my country and my position, for I am no foreigner, and do not represent another country. I am just a plain, ordinary American, temporarily called to Washington to look after the conduct of Uncle Sam's mints. My home is no more than California, with all the attractions I have truthfully described to you." She was disappointed, and soon found excuse to devote her attention to others present. It so happened that in taking our departure from the gathering we left the apartments at the same time with this lady and were the only occupants of the descending elevator, but she gave not the slightest indication either by word or expression of countenance that she had ever held conversation with me, or had even seen me before. What had been an interesting and amusing incident to me evidently was a matter of disappointment to her, and she could not resist the opportunity of exercising her womanly privilege of ignoring my presence. I certainly did not blame her.

The first twelve months or so in Washington passed most quickly. My time was so fully occupied with new and interesting duties, which with almost daily contact with the foremost men of the administration, as well as with many distinguished men who had business with the government, made my position highly interesting to me. I greatly enjoyed the opportunity to study at close range the characters of the men great in affairs, whose names were familiar to every citizen of our country, but of whom few people had any knowledge other than that pictured by the daily press, magazines, etc. After a while the novelty of all this wore off and there was more time to think of the dear ones and the old associates on the other side of the continent. In short, I began to long to return to our California home. I remember, when this feeling came on I wrote as follows to a friend who inquired how I liked my new position: "Washington is a most beautiful city and lovely place to live in, and there are lots of nice people here who do everything they can to make it pleasant for strangers like us. Nevertheless, they do not fill the places of friends and associates of a lifetime, and I must confess that I have begun to look for the day when I shall be packing my grips for permanent return to the Coast. Mrs. L. and Harry are ready to go any moment." However, the day did not come for some months following. In the summer of 1909 I received a telegram offering me the position of general manager of the People's Water Company of Oakland, my home city, and this gave me the excuse I wanted to sever my connection with the government service. I tendered my resignation, which took effect on August 1 of the above year, making exactly twelve years devoted by me to mint work with Uncle Sam. In accepting my resignation, Secretary MacVeagh sent me a letter of such a nature as to make a pleasing finish of my service with the Treasury Department.

[THE END]

Index

A
Alexander the Great, 107
Anglo-California Bank, 95
Anne, Queen, 111
Armstrong, Lieutenant, 46, 53, 86
Associated Press, 61
Audubon, 105

B
"Bank of All Banks," 88, 89
Bank of California, 95
Bigelow, Doctor William Sturgis, 107, 108
Brady, Jack, 86
Brenner, Victor D., 110
Breuner Building, The, 86
Britannia, 111
Bureau of the Mint, 91
Burns, William J., 23, 24

C
Cabinet room, 103, 123, 124
Charles II, 111
Chronicle Building, The, 56
Civil War, 108, 117
Clark, Bert, 88, 90
"Columbus Discovering America," 106
Committee on Civil Service and Retrenchment, 90
Committee on Ways and Means, 114
Confederate Army, 108
copper alloy, 97, 100
Cortelyou, Mr., 96, 110, 114, 117, 121, 126
Crocker Building, The, 56
Crocker National Bank, 95

D
Daggett, Honorable John, 11
Daniels, G.B., 11
Denver Mint, 114
Dewey Monument, 42
Dornin, George W., 84
double eagle, 18, 100-103, 105, 109, 110
Duchess of Richmond, 111

E
eagle, 100, 105, 106, 109, 110
electrolytic method of refining, 8, 12, 18
Emporium Building, The, 44, 46, 67, 68, 86
England, 112
Evening Chronicle, 8

F

Federal Reserve Bank Act, 128
five-cent piece, 109, 112
Flying Eagle cent of 1857, 103, 106
Fort Miley, 46
Funston, General, 67

G

Government Printing Office, 122
Great Britain, 111
Greece, 99, 107, 111
Gregg, Wellington, 95

H

Hale Building, The, 86
half eagle, 107, 108, 109
Hallenbeck, Kenneth, 7
Hammill, Joe, 85
Hawes, T.W., 45
Hilborn, Congressman, 11

I

"In God We Trust," 104, 105, 109
Indian, 105, 106, 108, 109, 111, 112

J

Jacobs, Assistant Treasurer, 63, 87

K

Kerfoot, Lee, 24-27, 29, 32, 33
King, Homer S., 92, 95
Knowland, Congressman, 22

L

Leach, Abraham P., 8
Leach, Edwin R., 8
Leach, Frank Aleamon, 7, 8, 10, 85, 87, 88, 90-92
Leach, Frank Jr., 8
Leach, Harry, 8, 132
Leach, Mary Louise Powell, 8, 128, 132
Liberty, 111, 112
Lincoln, (Abraham), 110
Lincoln school, 51, 86

M

MacVeagh, Franklin, 126, 132
Mare Island navy yard, 62
McKinley, President William, 8, 11
Metcalf, Victor, 123
Metropolitan Temple, 51, 86
Mills, Clark, 111
Minerva, 111
Mining and Scientific Press, 20
Morrill, Senator, 111

N

Napa *Reporter*, 7
National City Bank, 89
National Guard, 54
New York sub-treasury, 113
Nye, Mr., 12

O

Oakland *Evening Enquirer*, 8
Odd Fellows' Building, 65

one-cent piece, 109, 110, 112
one-dollar gold piece, 112

P
Palmer, Mr., 38
People's Water Company, 8, 132
Perkins, George C., 11, 22, 91
Philadelphia Mint, 8, 100, 101, 103, 113, 118-120
Philippine coinage, 8, 12, 116
Pocahontas, 112
Potomac River, 120
Pratt, Bela L., 108
Puget Sound, 26

Q
quarter eagle, 107-109

R
Ramsay, Sir William, 118, 119
Recollections of a Newspaperman, 7
Red Cross Society, 73
Relief Association, 73
Republican party, 126
Richard, T.A., 20
Rock Creek Park, 104
Roberts, George E., 91, 93, 127, 128
Roberts, J.W., 66
Rome, 111
Roosevelt, Mrs., 108
Roosevelt, President Theodore, 8, 63, 73, 96, 99-104, 106-110, 113, 121-126
Root, Senator, 123

S
San Francisco Clearing House Organization, 92
San Francisco Earthquake, 8, 35
San Francisco graft cases, 23
San Francisco Mint, 8, 10, 17, 35, 60, 77, 93, 95, 113, 114
San Francisco sub-treasury, 59, 62, 88, 89
Saint-Gaudens, (Augustus), 100-106, 109
Santa Fe Company, 79
Schmitz, Mayor, 66
Selby Smelting and Lead Company, 30, 62, 89
Seymour, Captain, 115
Shaw, L.M., 87, 88
Southern Pacific Company, 79
Spreckels Market, Emma, 56, 86
St. Francis Hotel, 57
Standard Oil Company, 72
Star of the West, 7
Steinhart, I., 95
Stuart, (painter), 112

T
Taft, President, 113, 114, 125, 126, 128
Tawney, Mr., 114, 115
Taylor, (architect), 121
three-dollar gold piece, 112
Treat, Treasurer, 96

U
Uncle Sam, 113, 122, 131, 132
United States Appraiser's Building, 69
United States Army, 46

United States Assay Office in
  New York, 31
United States Assay Office in
  Seattle, 23, 24
United States Congress, 17, 22,
  23, 91, 97, 104, 105, 109, 113,
  114, 122, 123, 128
United States House of Representatives, 111, 114
United States Marshal, 115
United States Mint, 8
United States Senate, 11, 90, 111
United States Signal Corps, 64
United States Treasury Department, 63, 87, 91, 93, 96, 98,
  99, 110, 121, 132
University of California, 24

V

Vanderlip, F.A., 89
Victoria, 111

W

War Department, 73
Washington, (George), 112
Wells Fargo & Co., 115
Western Union Telegram Company, 61
White House, 107, 108, 123, 124
Windsor Hotel, 86
Wyon, (artist), 111

Y

Yukon River, 15